THE ORIGINS OF CIVILIZATION

THE ORIGINS OF CIVILIZATION

Edited by
WILLIAM H. MC NEILL
and
JEAN W. SEDLAR

NEW YORK
OXFORD UNIVERSITY PRESS
LONDON　1968　TORONTO

Printed in the United States of America

Preface

This collection of readings concerns the origins of civilization in the ancient Orient. We begin with sample legends of creation that answered the naïve and universal human question: How did the world begin? These stories stand as a sort of introduction to the entire survey of world history as well as to this particular book: a reminder of the cosmic questions to which the study of world history must direct itself, implicitly if not explicitly.

The main portion of the volume is organized around two themes: the nature of kingship and the relationship between men and gods. One group of readings presents Mesopotamian views on these two questions; the second does the same for ancient Egypt. In neither case can the spheres of the political and the religious be sharply separated without doing radical injustice to the way ancient men thought and felt. Nevertheless, in discussing any particular text, it is legitimate to make such distinctions ourselves as a matter of practical convenience, while underlining the obvious fact that the ancients failed to recognize any such separation between human and divine affairs. A good practice is, in fact, to focus attention first on the various royal roles and activities suggested in the Mesopotamian texts and then to go back over the same materials asking about the relation between gods and men. This procedure cuts with the grain of things if one accepts the idea, proposed by Thorkild Jacobsen,* that ancient Mesopotamians conceived their relationships with the gods by projecting their own political experience upon the skies. In the case of Egypt, the sequence of inquiry can profitably be reversed, since the political power and position of the Pharaoh depended very much on Egyptian ideas about immortality and the gods.

There are other lines of inquiry worth pursuing for the par-

* "The Cosmos as a State," Ch. V of H. and H. A. Frankfort *et al.*, *The Intellectual Adventure of Ancient Man*, Chicago: University of Chicago Press, 1946.

ticular texts reproduced here. The *Epic of Gilgamesh,* for example, lends itself to several kinds of analysis. It is the oldest extant epic poem, and Gilgamesh is the first known literary hero. It may be worth discussing the significance of these facts, as well as what it means for a society to accept and admire the heroic virtues illustrated by the figure of Gilgamesh.

Also useful is an examination of how the text of this epic has been reconstituted by modern scholars from the fragments of different versions. This can provide a valuable handhold for reflection upon the larger issue of the interplay between modern scholarly techniques and the vision of the human past we inherit —the sort of information presented about human origins in the textbook, for example.

In the Mesopotamian texts affinities with our own literary and intellectual heritage are easily recognized. Basic ideas about men's relation to the gods and to one another passed into the Hebrew tradition and from the ancient Hebrews to us. The links are much weaker between ourselves and the ancient Egyptians. Thus the magical ideas behind the Pyramid texts are very alien to us, indeed all but incomprehensible. Yet the central importance of life after death to the ancient Egyptians comes through clearly; and it is instructive to compare Pharaoh's easy immortality through incantation with Gilgamesh's failure to achieve eternal life even after heroic effort.

The respective fates of Pharaoh and Gilgamesh are symptomatic of a basic difference between the two river-valley civilizations. The Egyptians had full confidence in their magical control over the supernatural; the Mesopotamians never escaped profound anxiety in their relations with the gods. In the light of this difference, many of the contrasts between the two literary traditions and the two styles of civilization they represent become more intelligible.

Thus, for example, the complaints (*"Admonitions"*) of the Egyptian scribe Ipuwer proceed on the assumption that political order and social hierarchy are and ought to be natural, normal, and dependable. No Mesopotamian writer would have had such confidence. Similarly, the story of Sinuhe reflects Egypt's isolation from its neighbors: for obvious geographical reasons Mesopotamia was always in close contact with the rest of the world. It is

worth asking whether the Egyptians' confidence in the divine
order was created by geographical factors, which guaranteed an
almost regular flood and fertile fields relatively free of foreign
plundering, whereas the lack of these regularities caused Mesopotamians to take a less confident view of the human condition; or
whether other explanations are needed.

While opening the gates to an extremely broad question of geographical determinism like this, we should never lose sight of the
drastic limitations upon modern knowledge of the ancient past.
Uncertainties surrounding the interpretation of ancient texts and
fragments should not be forgotten. In particular, our inability to
read the few fragments of Indus script that have been recovered
by archaeologists prevents the use of literary materials for the
study of this, the third of the most ancient river-valley civilizations. It is worth considering the degree to which this fact limits
our knowledge of that ancient society as against what we know
or can infer about Mesopotamia and Egypt. Such comparisons
are greatly aided by the use of photographs of art objects discovered at Harappa and Mohenjo-daro, and by site plans of those
two cities.

Unfortunately, written original sources do not allow us to
approach the Indus civilization at all; nor does the contribu-
tion of archaeology and art to our understanding of ancient Egypt
and Mesopotamia come into focus here. This reflects historians'
traditional reliance upon words and texts, and is, perhaps, a
necessary restriction, given the customary limits of historical
scholarship and time. All the same, for those who can do so, systematic supplementation of these texts by photographs of art
works and of archaeological sites will be particularly rewarding
in studying this earliest period of recorded human history.

The editors particularly wish to thank Professor J. A. Brink-
man of the Oriental Institute of the University of Chicago for his
invaluable help in identifying many obscure Mesopotamian
terms. Our chronology for Mesopotamia follows that of Brink-
man, "Mesopotamian Chronology of the Historical Period," in
the Appendix to A. Leo Oppenheim's *Ancient Mesopotamia*. For
the Egyptian dates we are indebted to Professor Klaus Baer of
the Oriental Institute of the University of Chicago.

With minor exceptions, the texts in this volume have been reproduced just as they appear in our sources. The present editors have made no attempt to standardize spelling as between English and American usage or in the transliteration of foreign terms into English. Diacritical marks indicating linguistic distinctions in the original languages have been almost completely omitted as being of little interest to the general reader.

The editors have supplied numerous footnotes of their own in order to aid the non-specialist in comprehending these texts. In many cases, the notes or other explanatory material provided by the translator have been adapted for this purpose. Other notes have been added to identify terms or explain unfamiliar allusions, provide supplementary background information, call attention to particular items, or point out similarities or contrasts between the passage at hand and some other passage or source. Technical discussions and scholarly references have been almost entirely omitted.

Although the significance of brackets, ellipses, and other punctuation marks varies somewhat with different translators, for the Mesopotamian and Egyptian texts the system in general is as follows: Brackets indicate restorations made by the translator where the cuneiform or hieroglyphic text was broken or otherwise unreadable; parentheses indicate interpolations made by the translator to better explain the meaning. Doubtful translations and foreign words appear in italics or are followed by a question mark in parentheses. Three dots mark a place in the text which cannot be restored; a full line of ellipses indicates material omitted by the present editors. In the Brhadaranyaka Upanishad, the parentheses are the translator's; a few words in brackets have been inserted by the editors.

Chicago, Illinois   W.H.M.
June 1968

Contents

Maps

THE ORIGINS OF CIVILIZATION

I

Legends of Creation

Introduction to Enuma Elish

The epic *Enuma Elish*, so called from its first words ("When on high"), is our principal source of knowledge about Mesopotamian cosmology. In its present form, it is a glorification of the god Marduk and his part in the creation and organization of the world. The advancement of Marduk from his earlier position as merely the patron deity of Babylon to supremacy over all the gods of Mesopotamia needed to be explained and justified; and the epic does this by attributing to him the defeat of Tiamat and the principal role in the creation of the universe. The city of Babylon is likewise singled out for special praise: it is said to have been founded at the very beginning of time as a residence for Marduk and the other gods. Thus in addition to being a religious explanation of the origin of the world, the epic is a political treatise.

In view of the prominence given to Marduk in *Enuma Elish* and the attempt to justify his and his city's supremacy, it appears likely that the poem was composed during the period when the rulers of Babylon first acquired hegemony over all Mesopotamia. This occurred under the First Dynasty of Babylon (1894-1595 B.C.), the dynasty of Hammurabi. We do not know when the epic was first committed to writing; all portions of it which have come to light post-date Hammurabi by many centuries. Of the principal extant fragments, the oldest (from Ashur) date back only to about 1000 B.C.; others were produced in the seventh or sixth centuries B.C.; but all are copies of more ancient originals.

Indeed, there is no doubt that the poem is based largely upon the cosmology of the Sumerians and that originally its chief figure was the head of the Sumerian pantheon, the god Enlil. According to Sumerian belief, earth and heaven are held apart by the atmosphere; thus it was Enlil, the god of the air, who had originally separated them from the primeval world matter. In fact, the names of all the gods participating in the creation (except for Tiamat), the monsters borne by Tiamat, and the winds created by Marduk are Sumerian in origin.

The epic was clearly intended for public presentation. Its form

3

is typical of Sumerian unrhymed poetry, consisting of couplets in which the second line usually forms a contrast, parallel, or supplement to the first. Every year on the fourth day of the New Year's festival the poem was recited by the high priest (and perhaps in part dramatized) before Marduk's statue. The purpose of the performance was probably to assure Marduk's good will; for this was the time when the gods determined the destinies of the land for the year to come.

Scholars have long been aware of the numerous similarities between the account of creation in *Enuma Elish* and that in the Book of Genesis. Both versions begin with a primeval darkness. In each case, the earth is created out of a watery chaos through a process of separation; even the words for this water (the Biblical "deep") are linguistically related: Tiamat corresponds to the Hebrew *tehom*. The order of creation is the same: light comes into existence and day and night are established prior to the formation of the heavenly bodies; the sky (firmament) is formed to separate the waters above and below; then the sun, moon, and stars are created in order to regulate and divide time. The culmination of the process in both versions is the creation of mankind.

The differences between the two accounts reflect the differences in basic theology between Babylonia and Israel. While the Book of Genesis knows but one God, *Enuma Elish* exhibits a multiplicity of deities personifying the various forces of nature. In the Babylonian story, several gods participate in creation: Apsu and Tiamat are the parents of the gods; Ea forms the subterranean sea out of the carcass of Apsu; and finally, after part of the universe has already taken shape, Marduk appears to complete the work by creating Heaven and earth, the heavenly bodies, vegetation, and (together with Ea) mankind.

The God of the Hebrews is distinct from matter: he creates out of nothing by the mere force of his command. To the Babylonians, on the contrary, matter was eternal; they could not imagine a time when only God was. Tiamat in *Enuma Elish* is both the primeval waters and a mythical personality; the earth and the things upon the earth are created out of her body. Marduk, the chief creator, is a solar deity who gives forth light; in Genesis light is a creation of God and not one of his attributes. The gods in the Babylonian story create through physical effort; the Hebrew God requires only his command. Indeed, in the Babylonian epic creation is somewhat incidental; the main body of the work deals with the conflict among the gods and the glorification of Marduk.

The position of man in the two versions is likewise dissimilar. In the Babylonian view, mankind was produced in order to conciliate the defeated gods, who otherwise would have been obliged to serve the victors; this service is now imposed upon man. There is also no place in the Babylonian account for a fall from innocence through free choice. Man was produced out of the body of the mother of the gods. His characteristics, like those of the gods themselves, have been from the beginning both good and evil.

ENUMA ELISH

Tablet I

When on high the heaven had not been named,[1]
Firm ground below had not been called by name,
Naught but primordial Apsu, their begetter,
(And) Mummu[2] Tiamat, she who bore them all,
Their waters commingling as a single body;[3]   5
No reed hut had been matted, no marsh land had appeared,
When no gods whatever had been brought into being,
Uncalled by name, their destinies undetermined—
Then it was that the gods were formed within them.[4]
Lahmu and Lahamu were brought forth, by name they were
        called   10
Before they had grown in age and stature.
Anshar and Kishar were formed, surpassing the others.
They prolonged the days, added on the years.[5]
Anu was their heir, of his fathers the rival;

From *Ancient Near Eastern Texts Relating to the Old Testament*, J. B. Pritchard, ed., E. A. Speiser, trans. 2nd ed., Princeton, Princeton University Press, 1950, 1955, pp. 60-69. Copyright 1950, 1955 by Princeton University Press. Reprinted by permission. Titled "The Creaton Epic" in Pritchard's text.

1. I.e., created. According to ancient belief, power over a thing is acquired by pronouncing its name.
  For an explanation of the italics, brackets, parentheses, and ellipses used in the texts, see the Acknowledgments.
2. Perhaps an epithet in the sense of "mother," not to be confused with the vizier Mummu who is mentioned in subsequent lines.
3. I.e., the fresh waters (Apsu) and the salt waters (Tiamat) have not yet been separated.
4. Within Apsu and Tiamat.
5. I.e., a long time elapsed.

Yea, Anshar's first-born, Anu, was his equal.[6]   15
Anu begot in his image Nudimmud.[7]
This Nudimmud was of his fathers the master;[8]
Of broad wisdom, understanding, mighty in strength,
Mightier by far than his grandfather, Anshar.
He had no rival among the gods, his brothers.[9]   20
The divine brothers banded together,
They disturbed Tiamat *as they surged back and forth*,[10]
Yea, they troubled the mood[11] of Tiamat
By their *hilarity*[12] in the Abode of Heaven.
Apsu could not lessen their clamor   25
And Tiamat was speechless at their [*ways*].
Their doings were loathsome unto [. . .].
Unsavory were their ways; they were *overbearing*.
Then Apsu, the begetter of the great gods,
Cried out, addressing Mummu, his vizier: 30
"O Mummu, my vizier, who rejoicest my spirit,[13]
Come hither and let us go to Tiamat!"
They went and sat down before Tiamat,
Exchanging counsel about the gods, their first-born.
Apsu, opening his mouth,   35
Said unto *resplendent*[14] Tiamat:
"Their ways are verily loathsome unto me.
By day I find no relief, nor repose by night.
I will destroy, I will wreck their ways,
That quiet may be restored. Let us have rest!"   40
As soon as Tiamat heard this,
She was wroth and called out to her husband.
She cried out aggrieved, as she raged all alone,
Injecting woe into her mood:

6. Anshar's equal.
7. Another name for Ea (Enki), the god of the earth and water.
8. Ea was master both in the sense that he possessed exceptional strength and wisdom, and that he was able to subject the elder gods to his will.
9. Variant translation: his fathers.
10. Var.: assaulted their keeper.
11. Literally, the "belly" or inner parts.
12. Var.: moving and running about.
13. Literally, "liver."
14. Var.: Said with raised voice.

"What? Should we destroy that which we have built?   45
Their ways indeed are most troublesome, but let us
        attend kindly!"[15]
Then answered Mummu, giving counsel to Apsu;
[*Ill-wishing*] and ungracious was Mummu's advice:
"Do destroy, my father, the mutinous ways.
Then shalt thou have relief by day and rest by night!"   50
When Apsu heard this, his face grew radiant
Because of the evil he planned against the gods, his sons.
As for Mummu, by the neck he embraced him
As (that one) sat down on his knees to kiss him.
(Now) whatever they had plotted between them,   55
Was repeated unto the gods, their first-born.
When the gods heard (this), they were astir,
(Then) lapsed into silence and remained speechless.
Surpassing in wisdom, accomplished, resourceful,
Ea, the all-wise, saw through their[16] scheme.   60
A master design against it he devised and set up,
Made artful his spell against it, surpassing and holy.
He recited it and made it subsist in the deep,[17]
As he poured sleep upon him. Sound asleep he lay.
When Apsu he had made prone, drenched with sleep,   65
Mummu, the adviser, was powerless to stir.
He loosened his[18] band, tore off his tiara,
Removed his halo (and) put it on himself.
Having fettered Apsu, he slew him.
Mummu he bound and left behind lock.
Having thus upon Apsu established his dwelling,   70
He laid hold on Mummu, holding him by the nose-rope.
After Ea had vanquished and trodden down his foes,
Had secured his triumph over his enemies,
In his sacred chamber in profound peace had rested,   75
He named it "Apsu," for shrines he assigned (it).
In that same place his cult hut he founded.

15. Take it in good spirit.
16. Apsu's and Mummu's.
17. Literally, "caused it to be in the waters," i.e. the sweet waters of Apsu.
18. "His" refers to Apsu, not Mummu, who was only the vizier and thus
not entitled to a band, tiara, etc.

Ea and Damkina,[19] his wife, dwelled (there) in splendor.
In the chamber of fates, the abode of destinies,
A god was engendered, most able and wisest of gods.   80
In the heart of Apsu[20] was Marduk[21] created,
In the heart of holy Apsu was Marduk created.
He who begot him was Ea, his father;
She who bore him was Damkina, his mother.
The breast of goddesses he did suck.   85
The nurse that nursed him filled him with awesomeness.
Alluring was his figure, sparkling the lift of his eyes.
Lordly was his gait, commanding from of old.
When Ea saw him, the father who begot him,
He exulted and glowed, his heart filled with gladness.   90
He rendered him perfect[22] and endowed him with a
        double godhead.
Greatly exalted was he above them, exceeding throughout.
Perfect were his members beyond comprehension,
Unsuited for understanding,[23] difficult to perceive.
Four were his eyes, four were his ears;   95
When he moved his lips, fire blazed forth.
Large were all four hearing organs,
And the eyes, in like number, scanned all things.
He was the loftiest of the gods, surpassing was his stature;
His members were enormous, he was exceeding tall.   100
"My little son, my little son!
My son, the Sun! Sun of the heavens!"
Clothed with the halo of ten gods, he was strong to the utmost,
As their awesome flashes were heaped upon him.
Anu brought forth and begot the fourfold wind   105
Consigning to its power the *leader of the host*.[24]

19. The Assyrian versions of this epic substitute here and elsewhere Lahmu and Lahamu for the Babylonian Ea and Damkina.
20. Here, the deep.
21. Here, the Assyrian versions replace Marduk's name by that of Ashur, chief god of Assyria.
22. A technical term referring primarily to the craftsman's final inspection of his work before pronouncing it finished.
23. I.e., unsuited to human understanding.
24. The host of monsters which Tiamat will soon create (lines 132-5 of this tablet).

He fashioned . . . , *station[ed]* the whirlwind,
He produced streams to disturb Tiamat.
The gods, given no rest, *suffer in* the storm.
Their heart(s) having plotted evil,   110
To Tiamat, their mother, said:
"When they slew Apsu, thy consort,
Thou didst not aid him but remained still.
When the dread fourfold wind he[25] created,
Thy vitals were diluted and so we can have no rest.   115
Let Apsu, thy consort, be in thy mind[26]
And Mummu, who has been vanquished! Thou art left
      alone!
[. . .] thou pacest about distraught,
[. . . without ce]ase. Thou dost not love us!
[. . .] pinched are our eyes,   120
[. . .]without cease. Let us have rest!
[. . . *to batt]le*. Do thou avenge them!
[. . .] and render (them) as the wind!"
[When] Tiamat [heard] (these) words, she was pleased:
"[. . .] you have given. Let us make *monsters*,   125
[. . .] and the gods in the mid[st . . .].
[. . . let us do] battle and against the gods [. . .]!"
They thronged and marched at the side of Tiamat.
Enraged, they plot without cease night and day,
They are set for combat, growling, raging,   130
They form a council to prepare for the fight.
Mother Hubur,[27] she who fashions all things,
Added matchless weapons, bore monster-serpents,
Sharp of tooth, unsparing of *fang*.
[With venom] for blood she has filled their bodies.   135
Roaring dragons she has clothed with terror,
Has crowned them with haloes, making them like gods,
So that he who beholds them shall perish abjectly,
(And) that, with their bodies reared up, none might turn [them
      back].[28]

25. Evidently Anu.
26. Literally, "heart."
27. Another name for Tiamat.
28. Literally, "turn back their breasts."

She set up the Viper, the Dragon, and the *Sphinx*,   140
The Great-Lion, the Mad-Dog, and the Scorpion-Man,
Mighty lion-demons, the Dragon-Fly, the Centaur—
Bearing weapons that spare not, fearless in battle.
Firm were her decrees, past withstanding were they.
Withal eleven of this kind she brought [forth].   145
From among the gods, her first-born, who formed [her
     Assembly],
She elevated Kingu, made him chief among them.
The leading of the ranks, command of the Assembly,
The raising of weapons for the encounter, advancing to
     combat,
In battle the command-in-chief—   150
These to his hand she entrusted as she seated him in
     the Council:
"I have cast for thee the spell, exalting thee in the
     Assembly of the gods.
To counsel all the gods I have given thee full power.[29]
Verily, thou art supreme, my only consort art thou!
Thy utterance shall prevail over all the Anunnaki!"[30]   155
She gave him the Tablets of Fate, fastened on his breast:
"As for thee, thy command shall be unchangeable,
     [Thy word] shall endure!"
As soon as Kingu was elevated, possessed of [the rank of Anu],
For the gods, his[31] sons, [they[32] decreed] the fate:
"Your word shall make the fire subside,   160
Shall humble the 'Power-Weapon,' so potent in (its) *sweep!*"

Tablet II

When Tiamat had thus lent import to her handiwork,
She prepared for battle against the gods, her offspring.
To avenge Apsu, Tiamat wrought evil.
That she was girding for battle, was divulged to Ea.
As soon as Ea heard of this matter,   5

29. I.e., dominion over all the gods.
30. The seven judges of the underworld.
31. Probably: *her* sons, i.e., the gods who had gone over to Tiamat's side.
32. Kingu and Tiamat.

He lapsed into dark silence and sat right still.
Then, on further thought, his anger subsided,
To Anshar, his (fore)father he betook himself.
When he came before his grandfather, Anshar,
All that Tiamat had plotted to him he repeated: 10
"My father, Tiamat, she who bore us, detests us.
She has set up the Assembly[33] and is furious with rage.
All the gods have rallied to her;
Even those whom you brought forth march at her side.
They throng and march at the side of Tiamat,   15
Enraged, they plot without cease night and day.
They are set for combat, growling, raging,
They have formed a council to prepare for the fight.
Mother Hubur, she who fashions all things,
Has added matchless weapons, has born monster-serpents,   20
Sharp of tooth, unsparing of *fang*.
With venom for blood she has filled their bodies.
Roaring dragons she has clothed with terror,
Has crowned them with haloes, making them like gods,
So that he who beholds them shall perish abjectly,   25
(And) that, with their bodies reared up, none might turn them
    back.
She has set up the Viper, the Dragon, and the *Sphinx*,
The Great-Lion, the Mad-Dog, and the Scorpion-Man,
Mighty lion-demons, the Dragon-Fly, the Centaur—
Bearing weapons that spare not, fearless in battle.   30
Firm are her decrees, past withstanding are they.
Withal eleven of this kind she has brought forth.
From among the gods, her first-born, who formed her Assembly,
She has elevated Kingu, has made him chief among them.
The leading of the ranks, command of the Assembly,   35
The raising of weapons for the encounter, advancing to combat,
In battle the command-in-chief—
These to his hands [she entrusted] as she seated him in
    the Council:
'[I have cast the spell] for thee, exalting thee in the Assembly
    of the gods.

33. The council of the gods which decided events upon earth.

[To counsel all the] gods [I have given thee] full power.   40
[Verily, thou art supreme, my only consort] art thou!
[Thy utterance shall prevail over all the Anun] naki!'
[She has given him the Tablets of Fate, fastened on his breast]:
'[As for thee, thy command shall be unchangeable], Thy word
    shall endure!'
[As soon as Kingu was elevated], possessed of the rank of Anu,[34]   45
[For the gods, her sons, they decreed the fate:
'[Your word] shall make the fire subside,
Shall humble the "Power-Weapon," [so potent in (its) *sweep*!]' "
[When Anshar heard that Tiamat] was sorely troubled,
[He smote his loins and] bit his lips.[35]   50
[Gloomy was his heart], restless his mood.
[He *covered*] his [*mouth*] to stifle his outcry:
"[. . .] battle.
[The weapon thou hast made], up, bear thou!
[*Lo*, Mummu and] Apsu thou didst slay.   55
[Now, slay thou Kin]gu, who marches before her.
[. . .] wisdom."
[Answered the counselor of] the gods, Nudimmud.

(The reply of Ea-Nudimmud is lost in the break from line 59 to
line 72. Apparently Ea had no remedy, for Anshar next turns to
Anu:)

[To Anu,] his son, [a word] he addressed:
"[. . .]this, the most puissant of heroes,
Whose strength [is outstanding], past resisting his onslaught.
[Go] and stand thou up to Tiamat,   75
That her mood [be calmed], that her heart expand.
[If] she will not hearken to thy word,
Then tell her our [word], that she might be calmed."
When [he heard] the command of his father, Anshar,
[He made straight] for her way, following the road to her.   80
[But when Anu was near (enough)] to see the plan of Tiamat,
[He was not able to face her and] he turned back.
[He came abjectly to his father], Anshar.

34. I.e., received supreme dominion. Anu was at one time the highest-rank-
ing god in the pantheon.
35. Signs of distress or anger.

[*As though he were* Tiamat[36] thus he] addressed him:
"My hand [suffi]ces not for me to subdue thee."   85
Speechless was Anshar as he stared at the ground,
Hair on edge, shaking his head at Ea.
All the Anunnaki gathered at that place;
Their lips closed tight, [they sat] in silence.
"No god" (thought they) "can go [to *battle* and],   90
Facing Tiamat, escape [with his life]."
Lord Anshar, father of the gods, [rose up] in grandeur,
And having pondered in his heart, he [said to the Anunnaki]:
"He whose [strength] is potent shall be [our] avenger,
He who is *keen* in battle, Marduk, the hero!"   95
Ea called [Marduk] to his place of seclusion.
[Giv]ing counsel, he told him what was in his heart.
"O Marduk, consider my advice. Hearken to thy father,
For thou art my son who comforts his[37] heart.
When facing Anshar, approach as though in combat;   100
Stand up as thou speakest; seeing thee, he will grow restful."
The lord[38] rejoiced at the word of his father;
He approached and stood up facing Anshar.
When Anshar saw him, his heart filled with joy.
He kissed his lips, his (own) gloom dispelled.   105
"[Anshar], be not muted; open wide thy lips.
I will go and attain thy heart's desire.
[Anshar], be not muted; open wide thy lips.
I will go and attain thy heart's desire!
What male is it who has pressed his fight against thee?   110
[*it is but*] Tiamat, a woman, that flies at thee with weapons!
[O my father-]creator, be glad and rejoice;
The neck of Tiamat thou shalt soon tread upon!
[O my father-]creator, be glad and rejoice;
[The neck] of Tiamat thou shalt soon tread upon!"   115
"My son, (thou) who knowest all wisdom,
Calm [Tiamat] with thy holy spell.
On the storm-ch[ariot] proceed with all speed.

36. The grammar and context of the original make clear that Anu's statement to Anshar is an exact quotation of Anu's previous speech to Tiamat.
37. I.e., his father's heart.
38. Marduk.

From her [*presence*] they shall not drive (thee)! Turn (*them*)
    back!"
The lord [*rejoiced*] at the word of his father.   120
His heart exulting, he said to his father:
"Creator of the gods, destiny of the great gods,[39]
If I indeed, as your avenger,
Am to vanquish Tiamat and save your lives,
Set up the Assembly, proclaim supreme my destiny!   125
When jointly in Ubshukinna[40] you have sat down rejoicing,
Let my word, instead of you, determine the fates.[41]
Unalterable shall be what I may bring into being;
Neither recalled nor changed shall be the command of my lips."

Tablet III

Anshar opened his mouth and
To Gaga, his vizier, a word he addressed:
"O Gaga, my vizier, who gladdenest my spirit,
To Lahmu and Lahamu I will dispatch thee.
Thou knowest discernment, art adept at fine talk;   5
The gods, thy fathers, produce thou before me!
Let all the gods proceed hither,
Let them hold converse, sit down to a banquet,
Let them eat festive bread, poured[42] wine;
For Marduk, their avenger, let them fix the decrees.   10
Be on thy way, Gaga, take the stand before them,
And that which I shall tell thee repeat thou unto them:
'Anshar, your son, has sent me hither,
Charging me to give voice to [the dictates] of his heart,
[Saying]: "Tiamat, she who bore us, detests us.   15
She has set up the [Assembly] and is furious with rage.
All the gods have rallied to her;
Even those whom you brought forth march at her side.
They throng and march at the side of Tiamat.

39. I.e., the one who determines the destinies of the great gods.
40. The Assembly Hall of the gods.
41. Marduk demands supreme authority in return for risking his life in combat with Tiamat.
42. This perhaps refers to the custom of mixing wine with spices before drinking it.

Enraged, they plot without cease night and day. 20
They are set for combat, growling, raging,
They have formed a council to prepare for the fight.
Mother Hubur, she who fashions all things,
Has added matchless weapons, has born monster-serpents,
Sharp of tooth, unsparing of *fang*. 25
With venom for blood she has filled their bodies.
Roaring dragons she has clothed with terror,
Has crowned them with haloes, making them like gods,
So that he who beholds them shall perish abjectly,
(And) that, with their bodies reared up, none might turn them
    back. 30
She has set up the Viper, the Dragon, and the *Sphinx*,
The Great-Lion, the Mad-Dog, and the Scorpion-Man,
Mighty lion-demons, the Dragon-Fly, the Centaur—
Bearing weapons that spare not, fearless in battle.
Firm are her decrees, past withstanding are they. 35
Withal eleven of this kind she has brought forth.
From among the gods, her first-born, who formed [her
    Assembly],
She has elevated Kingu, has made [him] chief among them.
The leading of the ranks, [command of the Assembly],
The raising of weapons for the encounter, ad[vancing to
    combat], 40
In battle the comm[and]-in-chief—
These to his hands [she entrusted] as she se[ated him in the
    Council]:
'[I have] cast the spell for thee, [exalting thee] in the
    Assembly of the gods.
To counsel all the gods [I have given thee full power].
[Verily], thou art supreme, my [only consort art thou]! 45
Thy utterance shall prevail over all the [Anunnaki]!'
She has given him the Tablets of Fate, [fastened on his] breast:
'As for thee, thy command shall be unchangeable, Thy word
    shall endure!'
As soon as Kingu was elevated, possessed of the rank of Anu,
For the gods, her sons, they decreed the fate: 50
'Your word shall make the fire subside,

Shall humble the "Power-Weapon," so potent in (its) *sweep!*
I sent forth Anu; he could not face her.
Nudimmud was afraid and turned back.
Forth came Marduk, the wisest of gods, your son,   55
His heart having prompted him to set out to face Tiamat.
He opened his mouth, saying unto me:
'If I indeed, as your avenger,
Am to vanquish Tiamat and save your lives,
Set up the Assembly, proclaim supreme my destiny!   60
When jointly in Ubshukinna[40] you have sat down rejoicing,
Let my word, instead of you, determine the fates.
Unalterable shall be what I may bring into being;
Neither recalled nor changed shall be the command of my lips!'
Now hasten hither and promptly fix for him your decrees,   65
That he may go forth to face your mighty foe!' ' "
Gaga departed, proceeding on his way.
Before Lahmu and Lahamu, the gods, his fathers,
He made obeisance, kissing the ground at their feet.
He bowed low as he took his place to address them: 70
"It was Anshar, your son, who has sent me hither,
Charging me to give voice to the dictates of his heart,
Saying: 'Tiamat, she who bore us, detests us.
She has set up the Assembly and is furious with rage.
All the gods have rallied to her,   75
Even those whom you brought forth march at her side.
They throng and march at the side of Tiamat.
Enraged, they plot without cease night and day.
They are set for combat, growling, raging,
They have formed a council to prepare for the fight.   80
Mother Hubur, she who fashions all things,
Has added matchless weapons, has born monster-serpents,
Sharp of tooth, unsparing of *fang*.
With venom for blood she has filled their bodies,
Roaring dragons she has clothed with terror,   85
Has crowned them with haloes, making them like gods,
So that he who beholds them shall perish abjectly,
(And) that, with their bodies reared up, none might turn them
    back.

She has set up vipers, dragons, and *sphinxes,*
Great-lions, mad-dogs, and scorpion-men, 90
Mighty lion-demons, dragon-flies, and centaurs—
Bearing weapons that spare not, fearless in battle.
Firm are decrees, past withstanding are they.
Withal eleven of this kind she has brought forth.
From among the gods, her first-born, who formed her Assembly, 95
She has elevated Kingu, has made him chief among them.
The leading of the ranks, command of the Assembly,
The raising of weapons for the encounter, advancing to combat,
In battle the command-in-chief—
These to his hands she has entrusted as she seated him in the
     Council: 100
'I have cast the spell for thee, exalting thee in the Assembly of
     the gods.
To counsel all the gods I have given thee full power.
Verily, thou art supreme, my only consort art thou!
Thy utterance shall prevail over all the Anunnaki!'
She has given him the Tablets of Fate, [fastened on his breast]: 105
'As for thee, thy command shall be un[changeable, Thy word
     shall endure]!'
As soon as Kingu was elevated, [possessed of the rank of Anu],
For the gods, her sons, [they decreed the fate]:
'Your word shall make the fire subside,
[Shall humble the "Power-]Weapon," so potent in (its) *sweep!*' 110
I sent forth Anu; he could not [face her].
Nudimmud was afraid [and turned back].
Forth came Marduk, the wisest [of gods, your son],
[His heart having prompted him to set out] to face Tiamat.
He opened his mouth, [saying unto me]: 115
'If I indeed, [as your avenger],
Am to vanquish Tiamat [and save your lives],
Set up the Assembly, [proclaim supreme my destiny]!
When in Ubshukinna [jointly you sit down rejoicing],
Let my word, instead of [you, determine the fates]. 120
Unalterable shall be what [I] may bring into being;
Neither recalled nor changed shall be the command [of my lips]!'
Now hasten hither and promptly [fix for him] your decrees,

That he may go forth to face your mighty foe!"
When Lahmu and Lahamu heard this, they cried out aloud,   125
All the Igigi[43] wailed in distress:
"How strange[44] that they should have made [this] decision!
We cannot fathom the doings of Tiamat!"
They made ready to leave on their journey,
All the great gods who decree the fates.   130
They entered before Anshar, filling [Ubshukinna].
They kissed one another in the Assembly.
They held converse as they [sat down] to the banquet.
They ate festive bread, poured [the wine],
They wetted their drinking-tubes[45] with sweet intoxicant.   135
As they drank the strong drink, [their] bodies swelled.
They became very languid as their spirits rose.
For Marduk, their avenger, they fixed the decrees.[46]

Tablet IV

They erected for him a princely throne.
Facing his fathers, he sat down, presiding.[47]
"Thou art the most honored of the great gods,
Thy decree is unrivaled, thy command is Anu.[48]
Thou, Marduk, art the most honored of the great gods,   5
Thy decree is unrivaled, thy word is Anu.
From this day unchangeable shall be thy pronouncement.
To raise or bring low—these shall be (in) thy hand.
Thy utterance shall be true, thy command shall be
          unimpeachable.
No one among the gods shall transgress thy bounds![49]   10
Adornment being wanted for the seats of the gods,
Let the place of their shrines ever be in thy place.[50]
O Marduk, thou art indeed our avenger.

43. The heavenly deities.
44. Literally: "what has turned strange?"
45. Such utensils often appear in pictures of banquets from this period.
46. I.e., made Marduk lord of the gods, in accordance with his demands.
47. Literally, "advising."
48. I.e., thy command has the authority of the sky-god Anu, who had formerly been the chief god.
49. Infringe thy prerogatives.
50. I.e., there will be a place for Marduk in their respective shrines.

We have granted thee kingship over the universe entire.
When in Assembly thou sittest, thy word shall be supreme.   15
Thy weapons shall not fail; they shall smash thy foes!
O lord, spare the life of him who trusts thee,
But pour out the life[51] of the god who seized evil."
Having placed in their midst a piece of cloth,
They addressed themselves to Marduk, their first-born: 20
"Lord, truly thy decree is first among gods.
Say but to wreck or create; it shall be.
Open thy mouth: the cloth will vanish!
Speak again, and the cloth shall be whole!"
At the word of his mouth the cloth vanished.   25
He spoke again, and the cloth was restored.[52]
When the gods, his fathers, saw the fruit of his word,[53]
Joyfully they did homage: "Marduk is king!"
They conferred on him scepter, throne, and *vestment*;
They gave him matchless weapons that ward off the foes: 30
"Go and cut off the life of Tiamat.
May the winds bear her blood to places undisclosed."
Bel's[54] destiny thus fixed, the gods, his fathers,
Caused him to go the way of success and attainment.
He constructed a bow, marked it as his weapon,   35
Attached thereto the arrow, fixed its bow-cord.
He raised the mace, made his right hand grasp it;
Bow and quiver he hung at his side.
In front of him he set the lightning,
With a blazing flame he filled his body.[55]   40
He then made a net to enfold Tiamat therein.
The four winds he stationed that nothing of her might escape,
The South Wind, the North Wind, the East Wind, the West
    Wind.

51. This expression is taken from the shedding of blood, which was considered the basis of life.
52. Since the Babylonians did not believe in creation out of nothing, it is unlikely that Marduk is described as destroying the garment in the absolute sense and then restoring it.
53. Literally, "outcome of his mouth."
54. Another name for Marduk.
55. Compare Exodus 19:18, where the Lord descends upon Mount Sinai in fire.

Close to his side he held the net, the gift of his father, Anu.
He brought forth Imhullu "the Evil Wind," the Whirlwind,
    the Hurricane,   45
The Fourfold Wind, the Sevenfold Wind, the Cyclone, the
    Matchless Wind;
Then he sent forth the winds he had brought forth, the seven of
    them.
To stir up the inside of Tiamat they rose up behind him.
Then the lord raised up the flood-storm, his mighty weapon.
He mounted the storm-chariot irresistible [and] terrifying.   50
He harnessed (and) yoked to it a team-of-four,
The Killer, the Relentless, the Trampler, the Swift.
Sharp were their teeth, bearing poison.
They were versed in ravage, in destruction skilled.
On his right he posted the *Smiter*, fearsome in battle,   55
On the left the Combat, which repels all the zealous.
For a cloak he was wrapped in an armor of terror,
With his fearsome halo his head was turbaned.
The lord went forth and followed his course,
Towards the raging Tiamat he set his face.   60
In his lips he held a spell;
A plant to put out poison was grasped in his hand.
Then they milled about him, the gods milled about him,
The gods, his fathers, milled about him, the gods milled about
    him.
The lord approached to scan the inside of Tiamat,   65
(And) of Kingu, her consort, the scheme to perceive.
As he[56] looks on, his[57] course becomes upset,
His will is distracted and his doings are confused.
And when the gods, his helpers, who marched at his side,
Saw the valiant hero, blurred became their vision.   70
Tiamat emitted [a cry], without turning her neck,
Framing savage defiance in her lips:
"Too [imp]ortant art thou [for] the lord of the gods to rise up
    against thee!
Is it in their place that they have gathered, (or) in thy place?"

56. Marduk.
57. Kingu's.

Thereupon the lord, having [raised] the flood-storm, his mighty
    weapon,   75
[To] enraged [Tiamat] he sent word as follows:
"*Why* art thou risen, art haughtily exalted,
Thou hast charged thine own heart to stir up conflict,
. . . sons reject their own fathers,
Whilst thou, who hast born them, hast foresworn love![58]
Thou hast appointed Kingu as thy consort,
Conferring upon him the rank of Anu, not rightfully his.
Against Anshar, king of the gods, thou seekest evil;
[Against] the gods, my fathers, thou hast confirmed thy
    wickedness.
[Though] drawn up be thy forces, girded on thy weapons,   85
Stand thou up, that I and thou meet in single combat!"
When Tiamat heard this,
She was like one possessed; she took leave of her senses.
In fury Tiamat cried out aloud.
To the roots of her legs shook both together.   90
She recites a charm, keeps casting her spell,
While the gods of battle sharpen their weapons.
Then joined issue Tiamat and Marduk, wisest of gods.
They strove in single combat, locked in battle.
The lord spread out his net to enfold her,   95
The Evil Wind, which followed behind, he let loose in her face.
When Tiamat opened her mouth to consume him,
He drove in the Evil Wind that she close not her lips.
As the fierce winds charged her belly,
Her body was distended and her mouth was wide open.   100
He released the arrow, it tore her belly,
It cut through her insides, splitting the heart.
Having thus subdued her, he extinguished her life.
He cast down her carcass to stand upon it.
After he had slain Tiamat, the leader,   105
Her band was shattered, her troupe broken up;[59]

58. I.e., you hate your own children.
59. The following lines divide Tiamat's forces into three categories: (1) the
gods who had gone over to Tiamat, (2) the eleven kinds of monsters which
Tiamat had created, and (3) Kingu, Tiamat's new husband and general.

And the gods, her helpers who marched at her side,
Trembling with terror, turned their backs about,
In order to save and preserve their lives.
Tightly encircled, they could not escape.   110
He made them captives and he smashed their weapons.
Thrown into the net, they found themselves ensnared;
Placed in cells, they were filled with wailing;
Bearing his wrath, they were held imprisoned.
And the eleven creatures which she had charged with awe,   115
The band of demons that marched . [. .] before her,
He cast into fetters, their hands [. . .].
For all their resistance, he trampled (them) underfoot.
And Kingu, who had been made chief among them,
He bound and accounted him to Uggae.[60]   120
He took from him the Tablets of Fate, not rightfully his,
Sealed (them) with a seal[61] and fastened (them) on his breast.
When he had vanquished and subdued his adversaries,
Had . . . the vainglorious foe,
Had wholly established Anshar's triumph over the foe,   125
Nudimmud's desire had achieved, valiant Marduk
Strengthened his hold on the vanquished gods,
And turned back to Tiamat whom he had bound.
The lord trod on the legs of Tiamat,
With his unsparing mace he crushed her skull.   130
When the arteries of her blood he had severed,
The North Wind bore (it) to places undisclosed.
On seeing this, his fathers[62] were joyful and jubilant,
They brought gifts of homage, they to him.
Then the lord paused to view her dead body,   135
That he might divide the monster and do artful works.[63]
He split her like a shellfish into two parts:
Half of her he set up and ceiled it as sky,
Pulled down the bar and posted guards.

---

60. The god of death. The imprisoned deities mentioned in lines 107-21 were not killed, however, but merely defeated.
61. This act insured the validity of documents in Mesopotamian society.
62. Anshar, Ea, and the other gods.
63. I.e., create various things out of the dead body of Tiamat.

He bade them to allow not her waters to escape.[64]   140
He crossed the heavens and surveyed the regions.
He squared Apsu's quarter,[65] the abode of Nudimmud,
As the lord measured the dimensions of Apsu.
The Great Abode, its likeness, he fixed as Esharra,[66]
The Great Abode, Esharra, which he made as the firmament.   145
Anu, Enlil, and Ea he made occupy their places.[67]

Tablet V

He constructed stations[68] for the great gods,
Fixing their astral likenesses as constellations.
He determined the year by designating the zones:
He set up three constellations for each of the twelve months.
After defining the days of the year [by means] of (heavenly)
    figures,   5
He founded the station of Nebiru[69] to determine their
    (heavenly) bands,[70]
That none might transgress or fall short.
Alongside it he set up the stations of Enlil and Ea.[71]
Having opened up the gates on both sides,[72]
He strengthened the locks to the left and the right.   10
In her[73] belly he established the zenith.
The Moon he caused to shine, the night (to him) entrusting.
He appointed him a creature of the night to signify the days:
"Monthly, without cease, form designs with a crown.
At the month's very start, rising over the land,   15

64. I.e., the waters of Tiamat contained in that half of her body from
which Marduk constructed the sky.
65. Or: placed himself opposite Apsu.
66. A poetic name for the earth, which the Babylonians visualized as a
dome over the Apsu.
67. Residences, not to be confused with the "stations" mentioned in Tablet V.
68. Paths.
69. The planet Jupiter.
70. The bands of the celestial vault.
71. The band of the north belonged to Enlil, the band of the south to Ea,
with the path of the planet Jupiter lying between them.
72. The mythological gates of the East and the West through which the
sun-god was believed to come out in the morning and depart in the evening.
73. I.e., Tiamat's belly, the center.

Thou shalt have luminous horns to signify six days,
On the seventh day reaching a [half]-crown.
At full moon[74] stand in opposition[75] in mid-month.
When the sun [overtakes] thee at the base of heaven,[76]
Diminish [thy crown] and retrogress in light.   20
[At the time of disappearance] approach thou the course of the
    sun,
And [on the twenty-ninth] thou shalt again stand in opposition
    to the sun."

(The remainder of this tablet is broken away or too fragmentary for
translation.)

Tablet VI

When Marduk hears the words of the gods,
His heart prompts (him) to fashion artful works.
Opening his mouth, he addresses Ea
To impart the plan he had conceived in his heart:
"Blood I will mass and cause bones to be.   5
I will establish a savage,[77] 'man' shall be his name.
Verily, savage-man I will create.
He shall be charged with the service of the gods
        That they might be at ease!
The ways of the gods[78] I will artfully alter.
Though alike revered, into two (groups) they shall be divided." 10
Ea answered him, speaking a word to him,
Giving him another plan for the relief of the gods:
"Let but one of their brothers be handed over;
He alone shall perish that mankind may be fashioned.[79]

74. *Sapattu*, "full moon," the prototype of the Sabbath insofar as injunctions against all types of activity are concerned.
75. With regard to the sun. This was a technical term in Babylonian astronomy. The first lunar opposition was at the full moon, the second when the moon stood between the earth and the sun just prior to the new moon.
76. The horizon.
77. *Lullu*, the word here translated as "savage," was perhaps a derivative of the ethnic term "Lullu," which the Babylonians associated with men of the dim and distant past.
78. Their positions and mutual relationships.
79. I.e., fashioned out of his blood.

Let the great gods be here in Assembly.   15
Let the guilty be handed over that they[80] may endure."
Marduk summoned the great gods to Assembly;
Presiding[81] graciously, he issues instructions.
To his utterance the gods pay heed.
The king[82] addresses a word to the Anunnaki: 20
'If your former statement was true,[83]
Do (now) the truth on oath by me declare!
Who was it that contrived the uprising,
And made Tiamat rebel, and joined battle?
Let him be handed over who contrived the uprising.   25
His guilt I will make him bear. You shall dwell in peace!"
The Igigi, the great gods, replied to him,[84]
To Lugaldimmerankia,[85] counselor of the gods, their lord:
"It was Kingu who contrived the uprising,
And made Tiamat rebel, and joined battle."   30
They bound him, holding him before Ea.
They imposed on him his guilt and severed his blood (vessels).
Out of his blood they fashioned mankind.
He[86] imposed the service and let free the gods.[87]
After Ea, the wise, had created mankind,   35
Had imposed upon it the service of the gods—
That work was beyond comprehension;[88]
As artfully planned by Marduk, did Nudimmud[89] create it—
Marduk, the king of the gods divided
All the Anunnaki above and below.[90]   40
He assigned (them) to Anu to guard his instructions.
Three hundred in the heavens he stationed as a guard.

80. The other gods who had gone over to Tiamat.
81. Literally, "ordering."
82. Of the gods, Marduk.
83. The prediction that Marduk would vanquish Tiamat.
84. Though Marduk addressed his question to the Annunaki, the Igigi furnish the answer, indicating that in this passage the normally separate Igigi (celestial gods) are included among the Annunaki (underworld gods).
85. Word meaning "the king of the gods of heaven and earth."
86. Ea.
87. I.e., the other rebel gods.
88. I.e., beyond human comprehension.
89. Ea.
90. Compare line 10 of this tablet, also note 84, above.

In like manner the ways of the earth[91] he defined.
In heaven and on earth six hundred (thus) he settled.
After he had ordered all the instructions,   45
To the Anunnaki of heaven and earth had allotted their portions,
The Anunnaki opened their mouths
And said to Marduk, their lord:
"Now, O lord, thou who hast caused our deliverance,
What shall be our homage to thee?   50
Let us build a shrine whose name shall be called
'Lo, a chamber for our nightly rest'; let us repose in it!
Let us build a throne, a recess for his abode!
On the day that we arrive[92] we shall repose in it."[93]
When Marduk heard this,   55
Brightly glowed his features, like the day:
"Like that of *lofty* Babylon, whose building you have requested,
Let its brickwork be fashioned. You shall name it 'The
     Sanctuary.' "
The Anunnaki applied the implement;
For one whole year they molded bricks.   60
When the second year arrived,
They raised high the head of Esagila[94] equaling Apsu.[95]
Having built a stage-tower *as high as* Apsu,
They set up *in it* an abode for Marduk, Enlil, (and) Ea.
In their presence he [96] *adorned* (it) in grandeur.   65
To the base of Esharra[66] its horns[97] look down.
After they had achieved the building of Esagila,
The Anunnaki *themselves* erected their shrines.
[. . .] all of them gathered,
[. . .] they had built as his dwelling.   70
The gods, his fathers, at his banquet he seated:

91. I.e., ways of the gods of the earth.
92. Arrive for the New Year's festival.
93. The sanctuary.
94. The temple of Marduk with its tower at Babylon.
95. This perhaps means that the foundation of Esagila reached down to the
waters of the Apsu.
96. Marduk.
97. The top of the temple tower was probably adorned with horns.

"This is Babylon, the place that is your home![98]
Make merry in its precincts, occupy its broad [places]."
The great gods took their seats,
They set up festive drink, sat down to a banquet.   75
After they had made merry within it,
In Esagila, the *splendid*, had performed their rites,
The norms[99] had been fixed (and) *all* [their] portents,
All the gods apportioned the stations of heaven and earth.
The fifty great gods took their seats.   80
The seven gods of destiny set up the three hundred [in heaven].

. . . .

When they had granted him the exercise of kingship of the gods,   100
They confirmed him in dominion over the gods of heaven and
    earth.
Anshar pronounced supreme his name Asar(u)luhi:[100]
"Let us make humble obeisance at the mention of his name;
When he speaks, the gods shall pay heed to him.
Let his utterance be supreme above and below!   105
Most exalted be the Son, our avenger;
Let his sovereignty be surpassing, having no rival.
May he shepherd the black-headed ones,[101] his creatures.
To the end of days, without forgetting, let them acclaim his
    ways.
May he establish for his fathers the great food-offerings;   110
Their support they shall furnish, shall tend their sanctuaries.
May he cause incense to be smelled, . . . their spells,
A likeness on earth of what he has wrought in heaven.
May he order the black-headed to re[*vere him*],
May the subjects ever bear in mind their god,   115
And may they at his word pay heed to the goddess.
May food-offerings be borne for their gods and goddesses.
Without fail let them support their gods!

98. May also be translated "which you love," virtual equivalents in the
Babylonian language.
99. Or "laws," pertaining to portents.
100. Meaning, "pronounce my name supreme."
101. Common metaphor for "mankind."

Their lands let them improve, build their shrines,
Let the black-headed wait on their gods.
As for us, by however many names we pronounce, he is our
    god![102]
Let us then proclaim his fifty names.

(The remainder of the epic enumerates at length fifty flattering
epithets which the gods have selected for Marduk.)

.   .   .   .

102. Just as human beings had patron deities, so Marduk was the patron of
the other gods.

Introduction to The Theology of Memphis

This remarkable document has attracted an extraordinary amount of
scholarly attention—largely because it appears to anticipate, at a
very early date, the Biblical Logos doctrine ("In the beginning was
the word," etc., from John 1:1). It has come down to us in a late
copy inscribed upon the so-called Shabaka stone, now in the British
Museum. The Pharaoh Shabaka, of the Ethiopian dynasty which
ruled Egypt 715-664 B.C., decreed that this ancient text, written
upon papyrus or some other perishable material, be copied onto
stone. It is unlikely that either the Pharaoh or his learned scribes
had any inkling of the actual age and significance of the document, though they recognized it as a "work of the ancestors" and
thus worthy of reverence. But its archaic language is evidence of its
antiquity; and the historical situation to which it refers occurred
only around the time of the union of Upper and Lower Egypt under
King Menes, about 3000 B.C.

Menes, founder of this First Dynasty, was a native of Thinis in
Upper Egypt; but he established Memphis as capital of the united
country. Correspondingly, the local Memphite deity, Ptah, soon came
to be regarded as chief of the gods of Egypt. Ptah was, besides,
the patron of artisans and craftsmen, so that it was not difficult to
regard him as the master craftsman who had created the world.

This theological drama, despite its Memphite origin, no doubt borrowed many of its ideas from the centuries-old speculations of the priests of Heliopolis, sacred city of the sun god, Re. In large part, Ptah merely appropriates to himself the characteristics of Re, usurping his prestige and his place in mythical history. All gods who had any part in creation are here regarded as merely the forms or aspects of the new chief god, Ptah. (A similar process occurred again under the Eighteenth Dynasty when Thebes became the capital of Egypt and its god, Amun, acquired the attributes of Re to become Amun-Re.)

The unusual feature of this Memphite theology, however, is that Ptah does not work in the ordinary physical way, as the sun god is supposed to have done. Ptah creates the world through the power of his mind or thought and through the speech which expresses his thoughts. The assumption is that thought is the source of all that exists, while speech is its agency. Thus the things of this world are merely the objective forms of thought.

The "Theology of Memphis" was intended, at least in part, for dramatic presentation. The beginning consists of short narratives interrupted by what seem to be dialogues between various gods, accompanied by phrases to indicate stage directions. The dialogues are often preceded by the hieroglyphic symbols for these gods, arranged facing each other as if to speak together. The end of the document is a philosophical discussion bearing no clear relation to the preceding drama, though it may have been intended as a narrative address to be delivered by some priestly orator. The central portion of the text—evidently the conclusion of the drama—has unfortunately been worn away. Before its discovery by archaeologists in the nineteenth century, King Shabaka's stone was used as a nether millstone for grinding flour by Egyptian villagers unaware of its true value.

THE THEOLOGY OF MEMPHIS

Live the Horus:[1] Who Prospers the Two Lands; the Two Goddesses: Who Prospers the Two Lands; the Horus of Gold: Who

From *Ancient Near Eastern Texts Relating to the Old Testament*, J. B. Pritchard, ed., John A. Wilson, trans., 2nd ed., Princeton: Princeton University Press, 1950, 1955, pp. 4-6. Copyright 1950, 1955 by Princeton University Press. Reprinted by permission.

1. The king of Egypt, here identified with the ancient sun- and sky-god, Horus.

Prospers the Two Lands; the King of Upper and Lower Egypt: Nefer-ka-Re; the Son of Re:[2] Sha-[ba-ka], beloved of Ptah-South-of-His-Wall, living like Re forever. His majesty copied this text anew in the House of his father Ptah-South-of-His-Wall. Now his majesty had found (it) as (something) which the ancestors had made but which was worm-eaten. It was unknown from beginning to end. Then [his majesty] copied [it] anew, (so that) it is better than its state formerly, in order that his name might endure and his memorial be made to last in the House of his father Ptah-South-of-His-Wall in the course of eternity, through that which the Son of Re: [Sha-ba-ka] did for his father Ptah-tenen,[3] so that he might be given life forever. . . .

The Ennead[4] gathered themselves to him,[5] and he judged Horus and Seth.[6] He prevented them from quarreling (further), and he made Seth the King of Upper Egypt in the land of Upper Egypt, at the place where he was (born), *Su.* Then Geb made Horus the King of Lower Egypt in the land of Lower Egypt, at the place where his father was drowned, Pezshet-Tawi. Thus Horus stood in (one) place, and Seth stood in (another) place, and they were reconciled about the Two Lands. . . .

Words spoken (by) Geb (to) Seth: "Go to the place in which thou wert born." Seth—Upper Egypt.[7]

Words spoken (by) Geb (to) Horus: "Go to the place in which thy father was drowned." Horus—Lower Egypt.

Words spoken (by) Geb (to) Horus and Seth: "I have judged you." Lower and Upper Egypt.

2. Egyptian kings were believed to be sons of the sun-god, Re.

3. Ptah-tenen or Tatenen: the name of Ptah as the primordial god, fashioner of all things.

4. A family of nine gods, in four generations: (1) Atum, the creator-god; (2) Shu, god of air, and Tefnut, goddess of moisture; (3) Geb, god of earth, and Nut, goddess of the sky; (4) the gods Osiris and Seth, and the goddesses Isis and Nephthys.

5. The earth-god, Geb (or Keb).

6. Reference to the legendary contest between the gods Horus (son of Osiris) and Seth, in which Geb decided which of them should rule Egypt.

7. Seth—Upper Egypt: apparently stage directions, perhaps meaning that the actor who played Seth was to go off toward the south. This portion of the text clearly was intended for dramatic purposes.

(But then it became) ill in the heart of Geb that the portion of Horus was (only) equal to the portion of Seth. So Geb gave his (entire) inheritance to Horus, that is, the son of his son, his first-born.[8] . . . (Thus) Horus stood over the (entire) land. Thus this land was united, proclaimed with the great name: "Ta-tenen, South-of-His-Wall, the Lord of Eternity."[9] The two Great Sorceresses[10] grew upon his head. So it was that Horus appeared as King of Upper and Lower Egypt, who united the Two Lands in Wall Nome,[11] in the place in which the Two Lands are united.

It happened that reed and papyrus were set at the great double door of the House of Ptah.[12] That means Horus and Seth, who were reconciled and united, so that they associated and their quarreling ceased in the place which they *reached*, being joined in the House of Ptah, "the Balance of the Two Lands," in which Upper and Lower Egypt have been weighed. . . .

The gods who came into being as Ptah:——[13]

Ptah who is upon the Great Throne . . . ;
Ptah-Nun, the father who [begot] Atum;
Ptah-Naunet, the mother who bore Atum;[14]
Ptah the Great, that is, the heart and tongue of the Ennead;
[Ptah] . . . who gave birth to the gods; . . .[15]

There came into being as the heart[16] and there came into being as the tongue[17] (something) in the form of Atum. The mighty Great One is Ptah, who transmitted [*life* to all gods], as well as (to) their *ka's*,[18] through this heart, by which Horus

8. Geb changed his mind, giving all of Egypt to his grandson Horus.
9. Names for Ptah.
10. The crowns of Upper and Lower Egypt.
11. The province (nome) of Memphis was named "White Wall."
12. The intertwining tutelary plants of Upper and Lower Egypt, symbolizing the union of the two parts of Egypt.
13. Or: "who have (their) form in Ptah."
14. Ptah was both Nun, the primordial waters, and his consort Naunet. In these capacities he brought forth Atum, the creator-god of the old Heliopolitan theology.
15. The text is badly broken at this point, though it is clear that three other forms of Ptah are mentioned.
16. Mind or intelligence was believed to reside in the heart.
17. The spoken word; the authoritative utterance.
18. *Ka*: the vital force, or personality.

became Ptah, and through this tongue, by which Thoth became Ptah.[19]

(Thus) it happened that the heart and tongue gained control over [every] (other) member of the body, by teaching that he[20] is in every body and in every mouth of all gods, all men, [all] cattle, all creeping things, and (everything) that lives, by thinking and commanding everything that he wishes.

His Ennead[4] is before him in (the form of) teeth and lips. That is (the equivalent of) the semen and hands of Atum. Whereas the Ennead of Atum came into being by his semen and his fingers, the Ennead (of Ptah), however, is the teeth and lips in this mouth, which pronounced the name of everything, from which Shu and Tefnut[21] came forth, and which was the fashioner of the Ennead.[22]

The sight of the eyes, the hearing of the ears, and the smelling the air by the nose, they report to the heart. It is this which causes every completed (concept) to come forth, and it is the tongue which announces what the heart thinks.

Thus all the gods were formed and his Ennead was completed. Indeed, all the divine order[23] really came into being through what the heart thought and the tongue commanded. Thus the ka-spirits were made and the hemsut-spirits were appointed, they who make all provisions and all nourishment, by this speech. (Thus justice was given to) him who does what is liked, (and injustice to) him who does what is disliked. Thus life was given to him who has peace and death was given to him who has sin. Thus were made all work and all crafts, the action of the arms, the movement of the legs, and the activity of every member, in conformance with (this) command which the heart thought, which came forth through the tongue, and which gives value to everything.

(Thus) it happened that it was said of Ptah: "He who made

19. The gods Horus and Thoth are equated with the organs of thought and speech. Thoth was the god of wisdom and the scribe of the gods.
20. Ptah, as mind and speech, has transmitted his divine power to all living things.
21. Atum's children. See note 4 above.
22. A distinction is made here between the act of creation by Atum in the ordinary physical way and the creation by Ptah through mind and speech.
23. Literally, "every word of the god."

all and brought the gods into being." He is indeed Ta-tenen,[24] who brought forth the gods, for everything came forth from him, nourishment and provisions, the offerings of the gods, and every good thing. Thus it was discovered and understood that his strength is greater than (that of the other) gods. And so Ptah was satisfied,[25] after he had made everything, as well as all the divine order. He had formed the gods, he had made cities, he had founded nomes, he had put the gods in their shrines, he had established their offerings, he had founded their shrines, he had made their bodies like that (with which) their hearts were satisfied. So the gods entered into their bodies of every (kind of) wood, of every (kind of) stone, of every (kind of) clay,[26] or anything which might grow upon him,[27] in which they had taken form. So all the gods, as well as their *ka*'s gathered themselves to him, content and associated with the Lord of the Two Lands.

The Great Seat,[28] which *rejoices* the heart of the gods, which is in the House of Ptah, *the mistress of all life*, is the Granary of the God,[29] through which the sustenance of the Two Lands is prepared, because of the fact that Osiris drowned in his water,[30] while Isis and Nephthys watched. They saw him and they *were distressed at* him. Horus commanded Isis and Nephthys *repeatedly* that they lay hold on Osiris and prevent his drowning. They turned (their) heads in time. So they brought him to land.[31] He entered the mysterious portals in the glory of the

24. The name of Ptah in his character as creator-god.
25. Or: "so Ptah rested."
26. Note that these images of wood, stone, or clay were not the gods themselves, but only places where the gods might appear.
27. I.e., upon Ptah in his form as the land rising out of the primordial waters.
28. Ptah's throne in his temple at Memphis.
29. The god is Ptah Ta-tenen, whose throne is the granary which keeps Egypt alive.
30. According to the most common version of this legend, the god Osiris was murdered by his brother Seth, who threw the corpse into the water. After a long search, Isis, his sister and wife, found the body and restored it to life. Thereafter Osiris reigned over the realm of the dead. The son of Osiris and Isis was Horus, who later contended with Seth for the rule over Egypt (see note 6 above).
31. Osiris was a god of vegetation. His rescue from drowning at this place is given as the explanation for Memphis's position as granary (i.e., capital) of Egypt.

lords of eternity, in the steps of him who shines forth on the horizon, on the ways of Re in the Great Seat.[28] He joined with the court and associated with the gods of Ta-tenen Ptah, the lord of years.

Thus Osiris came to be in the land in the "House of the Sovereign" on the north side of this land, which he had reached. His son Horus appeared as King of Upper Egypt and appeared as King of Lower Egypt, in the embrace of his father Osiris, together with the gods who were in front of him and who were behind him.

Introduction to the Vedas

The holy scriptures of ancient India are the Vedas, containing songs and sacrificial formulas, ritual directions, theological speculations, and hymns of praise to the various gods of the Hindu pantheon. The word "Veda" means "knowledge," signifying the knowledge of sacred, rather than worldly, things. Historically, the custodians of these texts were the Brahmin priests—indeed, the Vedas may be regarded as a kind of giant handbook for the religious ceremonies which it was the duty of the Brahmins to conduct. Even to the present day, pious Hindus consider the entire Vedas as revelation and every syllable in them as sacred and unalterable. As revelation—that which was received from a higher source and thus was not the work of any human being—the Vedas take precedence over all later religious literature, which is regarded as having only human authority.

The Vedas are divided into four collections (or *samhitas*): the Rig Veda, Sama Veda, Yajur Veda, and Atharva Veda. They are written in old Sanskrit (so-called Vedic Sanskrit), an Indo-European language having affinities with Greek and Latin and most modern European tongues. The Rig Veda is the oldest and the richest in content of the four Vedas; the Atharva Veda is the youngest, so much so that some sources count the Vedas as only three in number. The Rig Veda contains over a thousand hymns directed to various Hindu gods; the Sama Veda is a collection of texts for the songs sung by the priests at the sacrifice which formed the focal point of Hindu religious ritual; the Yajur Veda contains the sacrificial formulas, and the Atharva Veda various types of songs intended for magical purposes. To each of the four Vedas are attached additional texts later in date and somewhat different in nature from the basic *samhitas* (though the distinction is often not clearcut): *Brahmanas*—descriptions and explanations of the sacrifice, indicating that the ancient ritual was no longer accepted uncritically; *Aranyakas* ("forest books")—the ritualistic and allegoric meditations of ascetics who retired to the forests for contemplation; and *Upanishads*—treatises dealing with the ultimate meaning of the sacrifice and the basic problems of philosophy.

Having been created over a period of perhaps one thousand years (*ca.* 1500-500 B.C.), the Vedas lack any systematic structure or consistent system of thought. They were transmitted from generation to generation by learned *rishis* (wise men) who committed large portions of them to memory; thus it is not surprising that variant versions exist. The divergent Hindu sects emphasized those portions of the Vedas which conformed most nearly to their particular views; and the later philosophical schools were careful to support their (often contradictory) opinions by citations from appropriate Vedic texts. Thus, without ever losing their sacred character, the Vedas provided the basis and the authority for numerous and differing points of view, at the same time giving a fundamental continuity to Hindu thought.

The two hymns from the Rig Veda reproduced here present two views of the process of creation. In Hymn X, 121, creation occurs through the action of a god (Hiranyagarbha); but Hiranyagarbha is far from being the sole deity: note the repeated rhetorical question: "What god shall we adore with our oblation?" This attitude is not monotheistic: the worshipper may address his devotions to one god, but without doubting the existence of many other deities. Rig Veda X, 129, is perhaps the most famous of all Vedic hymns, showing a remarkably abstract and logical concept of creation.

FROM THE RIG VEDA

Book X, Hymn 121

1   In the beginning rose Hiranyagarbha,[1] born only lord of
    all created beings.
    He fixed and holdeth up this earth and heaven. What god
    shall we adore with our oblation?

2   Giver of vital breath, of power and vigour, he whose com-
    mandments all the gods acknowledge:
    Whose shade is death, whose lustre makes immortal. What
    god shall we adore with our oblation?

3   Who by his grandeur hath become sole ruler of all the
    moving world that breathes and slumbers;
    He who is lord of men and lord of cattle. What god shall
    we adore with our oblation?

4   His, through his might, are these snow-covered mountains,
    and men call sea and Rasa[2] his possession:
    His arms are these, his are these heavenly regions. What
    god shall we adore with our oblation?

5   By him the heavens are strong and earth is steadfast, by
    him light's realm and sky-vault are supported:
    By him the regions in mid-air were measured. What god
    shall we adore with our oblation?

6   To him, supported by his help, two armies embattled look
    while trembling in their spirit,
    When over them the risen sun is shining. What god shall
    we adore with our oblation?

7   What time the mighty waters came, containing the uni-
    versal germ, producing Agni,[3]
    Thence sprang the gods' one spirit into being. What god
    shall we adore with our oblation?

From *The Hymns of the Rigveda*, Vol. IV, R. T. H. Griffith, trans. and ed.,
Benares: E. J. Lazarus and Company, 1892.
   1. Literally, "the gold-germ," "source of golden light," the sun-god. In
later Hindu theology, Hiranyagarbha was identified with the world-creator,
Brahma.
   2. The mythical river of the firmament.
   3. The fire-god (compare the Latin *ignis*).

8   He in his might surveyed the floods containing productive
      force and generating Worship.[4]

      He is the god of gods, and none beside him. What god shall
      we adore with our oblation?

9   Ne'er may he harm us who is earth's begetter, nor he whose
      laws are sure, the heavens' creator,

      He who brought forth the great and lucid waters. What
      god shall we adore with our oblation?

10   Prajapati![5] thou only comprehendest all these created
      things, and none beside thee.

      Grant us our hearts' desire when we invoke thee: may we
      have store of riches in possession.

4. Or: creating the (ceremony of) sacrifice.
5. God of creation or life. Like Hiranyagarbha, he was later identified
with Brahma, the world-creator.

Book X, Hymn 129

1   Then[1] was not non-existent nor existent: there was no
      realm of air, no sky beyond it.

      What covered in, and where? and what gave shelter? Was
      water there, unfathomed depth of water?

2   Death was not then, nor was there aught immortal: no
      sign was there, the day's and night's divider.

      That One Thing,[2] breathless, breathed by its own nature:
      apart from it was nothing whatsoever.

3   Darkness there was: at first concealed in darkness this All
      was indiscriminated chaos.

      All that existed then was void and formless: by the great
      power of Warmth[3] was born that Unit.

4   Thereafter rose Desire[4] in the beginning, Desire, the pri-
      mal seed and germ of Spirit.

1. I.e., in the beginning. The non-existent (Sanskrit *asat*) has within it
the possibility of existence.
2. The single primordial substance, the unit out of which the universe was
developed.
3. Sometimes translated in this passage as "Austerity," meaning contemplation of the things that were to be created. The Hindus believed that
through contemplation and other ascetic practices great supernatural powers
could be attained.
4. Eros or Love (Sanskrit *Kama*), also considered a creative force.

Sages who searched with their heart's thought discovered the existent's kinship in the non-existent.

5   Transversely was their severing line[5] extended: what was above it then, and what below it?

There were begetters, there were mighty forces, free action here and energy up yonder.

6   Who verily knows and who can here declare it, whence it was born and whence comes this creation?

The gods are later than this world's production.[6] Who knows then whence it first came into being?

7   He, the first origin of this creation, whether he formed it all or did not form it,

Whose eye controls this world in highest heaven, he verily knows it, or perhaps he knows not.

5. A line drawn by the ancient sages (rishis) to make a division between the upper world and the lower, thus bringing duality out of unity—creating multiplicity out of the original One.
6. Note the subordinate status of the gods here—they are not creators, but are themselves created.

Introduction to the Brhadaranyaka Upanishad

Although portions of the Upanishads exhibit a high degree of philosophical abstraction and attach little importance to traditional religious practices, the following excerpt from the Brhadaranyaka obviously takes the ancient ritual seriously. The horse-sacrifice discussed here formed the central portion of the Vedic ceremony. The actions of the priest at the sacrifice were believed to reproduce the acts of worship by which Death (who may be identified with the god Hiranyagarbha) created the world. The Upanishad attempts to explain the creation of the world from the terms employed at the horse-sacrifice. The etymologies seem less fanciful when one remembers that words themselves were believed to possess a magical significance and actually lost their power if the priest failed to pronounce them correctly.

FROM THE BRHADARANYAKA UPANISHAD

Chapter I, Section 2

1   In the beginning there was nothing (to be perceived) here whatsoever. By Death indeed all this was concealed,—by hunger; for death is hunger. Death (the first being) thought, "Let me have a body." Then he moved about, worshipping. From his thus worshipping water was produced. And he said: "Verily, there appeared to me, while I worshipped (*arkate*), water (*ka*)." This is why water is called ar-ka. Surely there is water (or pleasure) for him who thus knows the reason why water is called arka [fire].[1]

2   Verily water is arka. And what was there as the froth of the water, that was hardened, and became the earth. On that earth he (Death) rested, and from him, thus resting and heated, Agni [fire] proceeded, full of light.

3   That being divided itself threefold, Aditya (the sun) as the third, and Vayu (the air) as the third.[2] That spirit[3] became threefold. The head was the Eastern quarter, and the arms this and that quarter (i.e. the Northeast and Southeast, on the left and right sides). Then the tail was the Western quarter, and the two legs this and that quarter (i.e. the Northwest and Southwest). The sides were the Southern and Northern quarters, the back heaven, the belly the sky, the dust the earth. Thus he [Death] stands firm in the water, and he who knows this stands firm wherever he goes.

4   He [Death] desired, "Let a second body be born of me,"[4] and he (Death or Hunger) embraced Speech in his mind. Then the seed became the year. Before that time there was no year.

From *The Upanishads*, F. Max Müller, ed. and trans. (Vol. I of *The Sacred Books of the East*), New York: The Christian Literature Company, 1897. The series was published by the Clarendon Press, Oxford, Eng.

1. Arka is the horse-sacrifice. The commentators disagree whether arka as used here refers to fire (especially, the sacrificial fire), or to water, from which fire is produced indirectly.
2. The three are Agni, Aditya, and Vayu.
3. Note how the horse used in the sacrifice is taken as representing the universe.
4. The second body is the year, or the annual sacrifice, the year being dependent on the sun (Aditya).

Speech bore him so long as a year, and after that time sent him forth. Then when he was born, he (Death) opened his mouth, as if to swallow him. He cried *Bhan!* and that became speech.[5]

5   He thought, "If I kill him, I shall have but little food." He therefore brought forth by that speech and by that body (the year) all whatsoever exists, the Rig, the Yajur, the Sama,[6] the metres, the sacrifices, men, and animals.

And whatever he (Death) brought forth, that he resolved to eat (*ad*). Verily because he eats everything, therefore is Aditi (Death) called Aditi. He who thus knows why Aditi is called Aditi, becomes an eater of everything, and everything becomes his food.

6   He desired to sacrifice again with a greater sacrifice. He toiled and performed penance. And while he toiled and performed penance, glorious power went out of him. Verily glorious power means the senses. Then when the senses had gone out, the body took to swelling, and mind was in the body.

7   He desired that this body should be fit for sacrifice (*medhya*), and that he should be embodied by it. Then he became a horse (*asva*), because it swelled (*asvat*), and was fit for sacrifice (*medhya*); and this is why the horse-sacrifice is called Asva-medha.

Verily he who knows him thus, knows the Asva-medha. Then, letting the horse free, he thought,[7] and at the end of a year he offered it up for himself, while he gave up the (other) animals to the deities. Therefore the sacrificers offered up the purified horse belonging to Prajapati,[8] (as dedicated) to all the deities.

Verily the shining sun is the Asvamedha-sacrifice, and his body is the year; Agni is the sacrificial fire (*arka*), and these worlds are his bodies. These two are the sacrificial fire and the Asvamedha-sacrifice, and they are again one deity, viz. Death. He (who knows this) overcomes another death, death does not reach him, death is his Self, he becomes one of those deities.

5. I.e., creation through the deity's exclamation.
6. The three elder Vedas. Note that they are created together with the universe and are not the product of men.
7. I.e., he considered himself as the horse.
8. A god sometimes considered as the creator of the universe.

Introduction to Genesis

The traditions upon which the Book of Genesis is based are obviously of great antiquity. The story of the creation, like other events in the history of the Hebrew people, was no doubt transmitted orally for many generations before being committed to writing. Tradition long held that Moses was the author of Genesis; but scholarship has since shown this to be impossible. The book as it now stands is a composite of various sources. The unknown author or authors sometimes included multiple accounts of the same event, and did not always resolve minor inconsistencies. It is now believed that three main sources were employed in the composition of Genesis: the "J" source, in which God is called "Yahweh" (Jahweh), originating in the tenth or ninth century B.C.; the "E" source, in which the word for God is "Elohim," slightly later in date; and the "P" or Priestly source, from about the fifth century B.C. The book as we now have it was probably substantially complete by the fifth century B.C.

According to the Genesis story, creation was effected by one God, who is eternal; creation was a purposeful event; and evil in the world is the punishment for disobedience to God.

FROM THE BOOK OF GENESIS
Chapter I

1   In the beginning God created the heaven and the earth.

2   And the earth was without form, and void; and darkness was upon the face of the deep.[1] And the Spirit of God moved upon the face of the waters.

3   And God said, Let there be light: and there was light.

4   And God saw the light, that it was good: and God divided the light from the darkness.

Genesis 1:1—2:25, King James Bible.

1. The earth was believed to rest upon a subterranean ocean.

5   And God called the light Day, and the darkness he called
Night. And the evening and the morning were the first day.
6   And God said, Let there be a firmament[2] in the midst of
the waters, and let it divide the waters from the waters.
7   And God made the firmament, and divided the waters
which were under the firmament from the waters which were
above the firmament: and it was so.
8   And God called the firmament Heaven. And the evening
and the morning were the second day.
9   And God said, Let the waters under the heaven be gathered
together unto one place, and let the dry land appear: and it
was so.[3]
10   And God called the dry land Earth; and the gathering together of the waters called he Seas: and God saw that it was
good.
11   And God said, Let the earth bring forth grass, the herb
yielding seed, and the fruit tree yielding fruit after his kind,
whose seed is in itself, upon the earth: and it was so.
12   And the earth brought forth grass, and herb yielding seed
after his kind, and the tree yielding fruit, whose seed was in
itself, after his kind: and God saw that it was good.
13   And the evening and the morning were the third day.
14   And God said, Let there be lights in the firmament of the
heaven to divide the day from the night; and let them be for
signs, and for seasons, and for days, and years:[4]
15   And let them be for lights in the firmament of the heaven
to give light upon the earth: and it was so.
16   And God made two great lights; the greater light to rule
the day, and the lesser light to rule the night: he made the stars
also.

2. The dome of the sky, which was believed to hold up the waters from
the face of the earth. In the time of the Flood "the windows of heaven
were opened. And the rain was upon the earth forty days and forty nights"
(Gen. 7:11-12).
3. The earth was believed to be flat, with four corners supported upon
invisible foundations.
4. In God's plan the heavenly bodies were merely lights, whereas many
pagan peoples believed they were deities to be worshipped.

17 And God set them in the firmament of the heaven to give light upon the earth.

18 And to rule over the day and over the night, and to divide the light from the darkness: and God saw that it was good.

19 And the evening and the morning were the fourth day.

20 And God said, Let the waters bring forth abundantly the moving creature that hath life, and fowl that may fly above the earth in the open firmament of heaven.

21 And God created great whales, and every living creature that moveth, which the waters brought forth abundantly, after their kind, and every winged fowl after his kind: and God saw that it was good.

22 And God blessed them, saying, Be fruitful, and multiply, and fill the waters in the seas, and let fowl multiply in the earth.

23 And the evening and the morning were the fifth day.

24 And God said, Let the earth bring forth the living creature after his kind, cattle, and creeping thing, and beast of the earth after his kind: and it was so.

25 And God made the beast of the earth after his kind, and cattle after their kind, and every thing that creepeth upon the earth after his kind: and God saw that it was good.

26 And God said, Let us[5] make man in our image, after our likeness: and let them have dominion[6] over the fish of the sea, and over the fowl of the air, and over the cattle, and over all the earth, and over every creeping thing that creepeth upon the earth.

27 So God created man in his own image, in the image of God created he him; male and female created he them.

28 And God blessed them, and God said unto them, Be fruitful, and multiply, and replenish the earth, and subdue it: and have dominion over the fish of the sea, and over the fowl of the

5. The word for "God" in this chapter is "Elohim," a plural noun. This use of the plural may be meant to indicate majesty and the totality of God's attributes, or perhaps that God is here consulting with the heavenly hosts.

6. In some pagan religions, certain animals, birds, or snakes were considered more important than man.

air, and over every living thing that moveth upon the earth.

29   And God said, Behold, I have given you every herb bearing seed, which is upon the face of all the earth, and every tree, in the which is the fruit of a tree yielding seed; to you it shall be for meat.

30   And to every beast of the earth, and to every fowl of the air, and to every thing that creepeth upon the earth, wherein there is life, I have given every green herb for meat: and it was so.

31   And God saw every thing that he had made, and, behold, it was very good. And the evening and the morning were the sixth day.

Chapter II

1   Thus the heavens and the earth were finished, and all the host of them.

2   And on the seventh day God ended his work which he had made; and he rested on the seventh day from all his work which he had made.

3   And God blessed the seventh day, and sanctified it: because that in it he had rested from all his work which God created and made.

4   These are the generations[7] of the heavens and of the earth when they were created, in the day that the Lord God made the earth and the heavens,[8]

5   And every plant of the field before it was in the earth, and every herb of the field before it grew: for the Lord God had not caused it to rain upon the earth, and there was not a man to till the ground.

6   But there went up a mist from the earth, and watered the whole face of the ground.

7   And the Lord God formed man of the dust of the ground, and breathed into his nostrils the breath of life; and man became a living soul.

7. A conventional phrase with which the compiler introduced the various sections of the book. Compare Genesis 5:1, 6:9, 10:1, etc.

8. This is evidently a second version of creation, in which the main purpose is to explain the origin of things.

8   And the Lord God planted a garden eastward in Eden;[9] and there he put the man whom he had formed.

9   And out of the ground made the Lord God to grow every tree that is pleasant to the sight, and good for food; the tree of life also in the midst of the garden, and the tree of knowledge of good and evil.

10   And a river went out of Eden to water the garden; and from thence it was parted, and became into four heads.

11   The name of the first is Pison:[10] that is it which compasseth the whole land of Havilah,[11] where there is gold;

12   And the gold of that land is good: there is bdellium and the onyx stone.

13   And the name of the second river is Gihon:[10] the same is it that compasseth the whole land of Ethiopia.

14   And the name of the third river is Hiddekel:[12] that is it which goeth toward the east of Assyria. And the fourth river is Euphrates.

15   And the Lord God took the man, and put him into the garden of Eden to dress it and to keep it.

16   And the Lord God commanded the man, saying, Of every tree of the garden thou mayest freely eat:

17   But of the tree of the knowledge of good and evil, thou shalt not eat of it: for in the day that thou eatest thereof thou shalt surely die.

18   And the Lord God said, It is not good that the man should be alone; I will make him an help meet[13] for him.

19   And out of the ground the Lord God formed every beast of the field, and every fowl of the air; and brought them unto Adam[14] to see what he would call them: and whatsoever Adam

9. The word means "delight." Some scholars identify Eden with Dilmun, which in Mesopotamian belief was the paradise lying somewhere in the distant East.

10. The location of the rivers Pison and Gihon is uncertain, though they may have been tributaries of the Tigris.

11. A region of Arabia, or possibly a people from Arabia.

12. The Tigris River.

13. Suitable.

14. The generic term for "man" in the Hebrew language. The Hebrew text has "the man" until Genesis 3:17, where "man" appears for the first time without "the."

called every living creature, that was the name thereof.

20 And Adam gave names to all cattle, and to the fowl of the air, and to every beast of the field; but for Adam there was not found an help meet for him.

21 And the Lord God caused a deep sleep to fall upon Adam, and he slept; and he took one of his ribs, and closed up the flesh instead thereof;

22 And the rib, which the Lord God had taken from man, made he a woman, and brought her unto the man.

23 And Adam said, This is now bone of my bones, and flesh of my flesh: she shall be called Woman, because she was taken out of Man.

24 Therefore shall a man leave his father and his mother, and shall cleave unto his wife: and they shall be one flesh.

25 And they were both naked, the man and his wife, and were not ashamed.

II

Mesopotamian Civilization

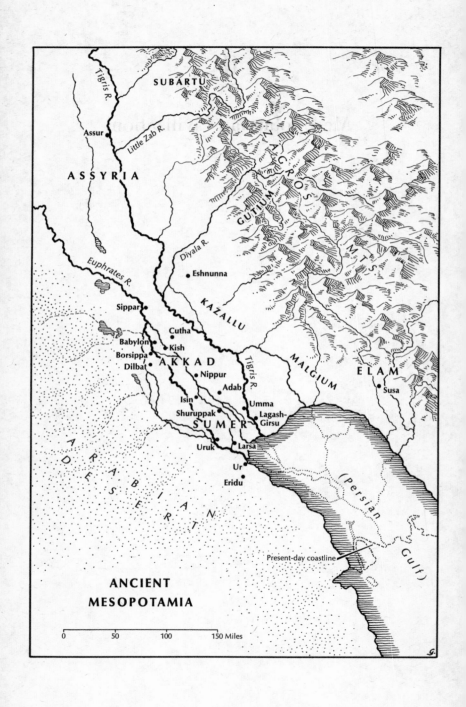

ANCIENT
MESOPOTAMIA

SUBARTU

Tigris R.

Little Zab R.

Assur

ASSYRIA

Euphrates R.

Sippar

Cutha

Babylon

Kish

Borsippa

AKKAD

Dilbat

Nippur

Adab

Isin

Shuruppak

SUMER

Uruk

Larsa

Ur

Eridu

ZAGROS

GUTIUM

Diyala R.

Eshnunna

KAZALLU

Tigris R.

MALGIUM

ELAM

Susa

Umma

Lagash-
Girsu

MTS.

ARABIAN DESERT

(Persian

Gulf)

Present-day coastline

0   50   100   150 Miles

Introduction to Lugalzaggisi, King of Erech

Lugalzaggisi, who reigned about 2350 B.C., began his political career as ruler of the city of Umma—a position he evidently usurped, since he was not descended from the previous royal line. From there he went on to conquer Lagash, whose rivalry with Umma dated back at least two centuries. An account of the sack of Lagash is preserved in the inscriptions of her reformer king, Urukagina, who complained bitterly against Lugalzaggisi's sacrilege in plundering and burning the temples. Lugalzaggisi's next step was the conquest of Uruk (Erech), formerly the seat of an important dynasty, to which he moved his capital. Evidently he sought to legitimate his power throughout the land of Sumer, for he took care to relate himself to the deities of each of the various cities he subjugated.

Though Lugalzaggisi boasts of conquering all the lands between the Mediterranean and the Persian Gulf, this cannot refer to much more than a raid, probably with the purpose of opening up trade routes. Within a few years after this exploit, the entire region became subject to a greater conqueror than he—Sargon, King of Agade.

LUGALZAGGISI, KING OF ERECH

To Enlil[1] king of countries Lugalzaggisi king of Erech,[2] king of the country, priest of Anu,[3] the exalted man of Nisaba,[4] son

Vase inscription and tablet from *Royal Inscriptions of Sumer and Akkad*, G. A. Barton, ed. and trans., New Haven: Yale University Press, 1929, pp. 97-101. Reprinted by permission of Yale University Press.

1. Chief executive of the Sumerian gods and god of thunder. See note 3 below.

2. The Biblical spelling for "Uruk," one of the oldest cities of Sumer, home of the legendary Gilgamesh, and mentioned in Genesis 10:10.

3. Chief god of the Sumerian pantheon, a sky-god and patron of the city of Uruk, Anu is the first Mesopotamian chief god known to historians. However, by the literary period he had become something of a figurehead, while

of Ukush, *patesi*[5] of Umma, the exalted man of Nisaba, looked upon by the favoring eye of Anu, king of countries, the great *patesi* of Enlil, endowed with intelligence by Enki,[6] whose name was named by Utu,[7] exalted messenger of Enzu,[8] the he-lion of Utu, the strong one of Ininni,[9] the son borne by Nisaba, nourished by the life-giving milk of Ninkhursag,[10] who is the divine prince, the priest of Erech, chief executive of Ninabukhadu,[11] lady of Erech, chief dignitary to the gods. When Enlil, king of countries, to Lugalzaggisi the kingship of the country had presented, when he before the land had established full justice, the countries his might had overthrown, from the sunrise to sunset he imposed tribute on them. At that time from the sea the lower the Tigris and the Euphrates to the sea the upper[12] his power fully established justice; from the rising of the sun to the setting of the sun Enlil . . . as a possession . . . took for him. The lands in safety reposed; the country was irrigated with the water of joy. In the sanctuaries of Sumer as *patesi* of the lands and in Erech as priest of the highest they appointed him. When Erech with gladness he had made bright, Ur[13] like an ox its head to heaven he raised, Larsa[14] the city beloved by Utu with waters of joy he watered; Umma[15] the city beloved by Shara[16] to great power he raised: Kininniesh[17] like a pregnant ewe in a watered enclosure he restored her fatness; the place of heaven

---

the actual powers of the office were exercised by his younger colleague, the god Enlil.

4. The goddess of grain, of scribes, and of wisdom; the patron of the city of Umma.

5. An old reading of the sign for *ensi* (governor).

6. The god of water and wisdom, patron of the city of Eridu, also called Ea.

7. Another name for Shamash, the sun-god.

8. A god, the son of Enlil.

9. A love-goddess of Lagash, also known as Inanna or Irnini.

10. Also called Nintu (or Nintud): a mother-goddess.

11. A goddess.

12. Upper and Lower Sea: the Mediterranean and the Persian Gulf.

13. Important city in the extreme south of Sumer, later the seat of the famous Third Dynasty of Ur.

14. A city of southern Sumer.

15. A city in central Sumer.

16. The god who regulated land-boundaries, the counselor and vice-regent of the god Anu.

17. A city of Sumer.

and earth to the height of heaven he restored. Lugalzaggisi, king of Erech, king of the country, the one sent of Enlil, king of countries, at Nippur[18] the offering of Ininni made abundant, pure water he poured out. . . . "Enlil, king of the lands,—may Anu whom he loves my offering pour forth, my life as life advance, cause the country in quietness to repose, people like the grass may he increase abundantly, the herds of Anu may he safely preserve, upon the country as a blessed land may he turn his eyes, a good fate may they allot, may they not alter it! The shepherd who lifts up the head of the ox may he be forever!" For his life to Enlil the king whom he loves, he presented it.

. . . .

Lugalzaggisi, lord of the land of Erech, king of the land of Ur. Whoever this inscription . . . destroys, may Enlil and Shamash[19] his foundation tear out, and his seed snatch away! Whoever this image . . . shall obscure may Enlil his name destroy, his weapon break! Before Enlil he set it up.

18. (Dur-ilu): a city on the boundary between Sumer and Akkad.
19. The sun-god, also known as Utu.

Introduction to Chronicles Concerning Sargon, King of Agade

The forebears of Sargon probably belonged to one of the semi-nomadic Semitic tribes that lived on the fringes of Mesopotamian civilization and occasionally came to settle in the towns. His obscure origin is illustrated by the story—a folklore motif found among various peoples—that as a baby he was cast on the river in a basket of rushes, then found and brought up by a lowly workman. Sargon claims to have begun his career as cup-bearer to the king of Kish, the great Semitic city which, according to the Sumerian King List, was the seat of the first dynasty to rule the world after the Flood. We do not know by what means he later carved out a personal domain for himself around the city of Agade (called "Akkad" in the Semitic tongue), a place apparently located not far from Babylon, though its ruins have never been discovered.

Sargon was the first great conqueror known to history. Agade was the starting-point and remained the center of his empire, giving its name not only to the entire region of northern Babylonia (Akkad), but also to the Semitic language spoken there (Akkadian). Sargon's first conquests seem to have been along the Upper Euphrates as far as Mari. He then marched into Assyria, sacking the city of Ashur, and went on to subjugate the Gutian tribesmen of the Zagros mountains. Turning southward, he defeated Lugalzaggisi, the overlord of Sumer, and advanced into Elam on the east. Westward he marched to the Mediterranean, overrunning Syria as far south as Lebanon.

The empire founded by Sargon lasted for over a century and a half (*ca.* 2330-2160 B.C.). His conquests were organized into provinces under governors either sent directly from the capital or chosen from some local family loyal to the sovereign. Sumer, the ancient land of civilization, was treated leniently, though we may suppose that the non-Semitic Sumerians nonetheless resented the domination of a foreign (and to them, less advanced) people. The control of Agade over the empire was never secure. Revolts broke out constantly, as the various subjugated cities and peoples sought to throw off an unwelcome yoke. In the last years of the Sargonid dynasty, Elam and much of Sumer became independent, while the Amurru (Amorites) of the western desert threatened the imperial borderlands. The final blow was the invasion of the Gutians; and Gutian kings ruled much of Babylonia throughout the following century.

CHRONICLES CONCERNING SARGON, KING OF AGADE

I

Sargon, king of Agade, through the royal gift of Ishtar[1] was
    exalted,
and he possessed no foe nor rival. His glory over the world

I and II are from *Chronicles Concerning Early Babylonian Kings*, L. W. King, ed. and trans., London: Luzac and Company, 1907, pp. 3-9, 87-94. Reprinted by permission. III and IV are from *Royal Inscriptions of Sumer and Akkad*, G. A. Barton, ed. and trans., New Haven: Yale University Press, 1929, pp. 101-7, 109-11. Reprinted by permission of Yale University Press.
    1. Goddess of love, daughter of the god Anu, known as Inanna to the Sumerians.

he poured out. The Sea in the East[2] he crossed,

and in the eleventh year[3] the Country of the West[4] in its full extent his hand subdued.

He united them under one control; he set up his images in the West;

their booty he brought over at (his) word.

The sons of his palace for five *kasbu*[5] (around) he settled,

and over the hosts of the world he reigned supreme.

Against Kasalla[6] he marched, and he turned Kasalla into mounds and heaps of ruins;

he destroyed (the land and left not) enough for a bird to rest thereon.

Afterwards in his old age all the lands revolted against him,

and they besieged him in Agade; and Sargon went forth to battle and defeated them;

he accomplished their overthrow, and their wide-spreading host he destroyed.

Afterwards he attacked the land of Subartu[7] in his might, and they submitted to his arms,

and Sargon settled that revolt, and defeated them;

he accomplished their overthrow, and their wide-spreading host he destroyed,

and he brought their possessions into Agade.

The soil from the trenches of Babylon he removed,

and the boundaries of Agade he made like those of Babylon.[8]

But because of the evil which he had committed the great lord Marduk[9] was angry,

---

2. Probably the Persian Gulf.

3. Probably the eleventh year of Sargon's reign.

4. Syria.

5. An old reading of the sign for *beru*. The Mesopotamians calculated distance according to walking time, so that a *beru* in mountainous country was shorter in actual mileage than one in the plains. One *beru* represented the distance a man could walk in two hours' time—about six and a half miles in level country. Five *kasbu* thus meant a good day's walking distance.

6. A region immediately to the east of Akkad across the Tigris.

7. A hilly region northeast of Akkad beyond the Tigris.

8. This perhaps means that he included both Agade and Babylon within the boundary of his kingdom, though more probably he increased the boundaries of Agade until they were as large as those of Babylon.

9. Chief of the Babylonian pantheon of gods.

and he destroyed his people by famine.
From the rising of the Sun unto the setting of the Sun
they opposed him and gave (him) no rest.

II

Sargon, the mighty king, the king of Agade, am I.
My mother was lowly, my father I knew not,
and the brother of my father dwelleth in the mountain.
My city is Azupiranu, which lieth on the bank of the Euphrates.
My lowly mother conceived me, in secret she brought me forth.   5
She set me in a basket of rushes, with bitumen she closed my
     door;
she cast me into the river, which (rose) not over me.
The river bore me up, unto Akki, the irrigator, it carried me.
Akki, the irrigator, with . . . lifted me out,
Akki, the irrigator, as his own son . . . reared me,   10
Akki, the irrigator, as his gardener appointed me.
While I was a gardener the goddess Ishtar loved me,
and for . . .-four years I ruled the kingdom.
The black-headed [people]s[10] I ruled, I gov[erned];
mighty [mountain]s with axes of bronze did I des[troy].   15
I bolted fast the upp[er] mountains;
I burst through the low[er] mountains.[11]
[The Country] of the Sea[12] three times did I besiege;
Dilmun[13] did . . .
[Unto] the great Dur-ilu[14] [I went up], I . . .   20
. . . I altered . . .
Whatsoever king shall be exalted after me,

· · · · · · · · · · · · · · · ·

let him [rule, let him govern] the black-headed peoples;
mighty [mountain]s with axes [of bronze let him destroy].   25
Let him bolt fast the upper mountains;

10. Frequent expression for the Mesopotamians.
11. Upper and lower mountains: identification uncertain, though "upper"
would indicate upstream and "lower" downstream.
12. Probably the marshy country around the mouths of the Tigris and Euphrates rivers.
13. A semi-legendary country, probably an island in the Persian Gulf, often
identified with the island of Bahrein.
14. Another name for the city of Nippur.

[let him burst through the lower mountains].
The Country of the Sea let him three times besiege;
[let Dilmun . . . .]
[Unto] the great Dur-ilu let him go up, and [let him . . .]   30
[. . .] from my city of Aga[de . . .]

.   .   .   .

III

Sargon king [of] Agade, overseer of Ishtar, king of Kish,
pašišu[15] priest of Anu,[16] king of the land, the great viceregent of
Enlil,[17] the city Erech[18] he subjugated, and its wall he destroyed; the men of Erech with mighty weapons he cut off: all
the fields he destroyed. Lugalzaggisi king of Erech was overthrown, his hand overpowered, in vile fetters, by the gate of Enlil he placed him. Sargon king of Agade with the man of Ur[19]
fought, all the fields he destroyed. His city he subjugated, and
its wall destroyed. The temple of Ninmar[20] he subjugated, its
wall he destroyed and all its country from Lagash[21] unto the sea
he subjugated. His weapons in the sea he washed. With the
men of Umma[22] he fought, all the fields he devastated, their city
he subjugated, and its wall he destroyed.

Unto Sargon, king of the land, the god Enlil gave, no one op-
posing, from the upper sea to the lower sea[23] Enlil gave unto him;
and from the lower sea the citizens (?) of Agade the viceroy of
. . . Uga, the man of Mari[24] and Elam[25] before Sargon, king of

15. Literally, "one who anoints," i.e., a category of priest.
16. Chief of the Sumerian pantheon, the sky-god and patron of the city of
Uruk (Erech).
17. The god of thunder, sometimes a destructive deity, but also the one
who brought abundance and prosperity, fashioned the plow and the ax,
made the day come forth, etc.
18. (Also known as Uruk); important city in southern Sumer.
19. I.e., king of Ur (city in the extreme south of Sumer).
20. A Sumerian goddess.
21. A city in southern Sumer which played an important political role for
over a century prior to the time of Sargon.
22. The Sumerian city which was the original home of Lugalzaggisi (see
preceding selection).
23. Upper sea: the Mediterranean. Lower sea: the Persian Gulf.
24. A city northwest of Akkad on the middle Euphrates.
25. Mountainous region east of the Tigris, now in southwestern Iran.

the land, stood. . . . Sargon, king of the lands of the earth, Kish[26]
—its place he restored; their city he made strong for them. Whoever this inscription destroys, may Shamash[27] his foundation
tear out, and his seed remove! . . .

IV

Sargon, king of Kish, thirty-four campaigns won, the walls
he destroyed as far as the shore of the sea, the ships of Melukha,
the ships of Magan, the ships of Dilmun,[28] at the wharf before
Agade he moored. Sargon, the king, in Tutuli[29] unto Dagan[30]
offered worship, the upper country he gave (him)—Mari, Yarmuti and Ibla[31] as far as the forest of cedar and the mountains
of silver. To Sargon, the king, the hand of Enlil a rival did not
permit. Fifty-four thousand men daily in his presence eat food.
Whoever this tablet destroys may Anu his name destroy, may
Enlil his seed extirpate, may Ishtar . . .

(The rest is broken away.)

26. City of northern Sumer, the capital for several important dynasties.
Rulers of Sumer were often given the title "king of Kish."
27. The sun-god.
28. Melukha, Magan, Dilmun: countries east of Mesopotamia, regarded as
distant and exotic, probably located along the Persian Gulf.
29. Somewhere northwest of Babylonia, perhaps as far as Mari. Three different places are known to bear this name.
30. An old Semitic agricultural deity worshipped first in Mesopotamia,
later in Syria and Palestine (e.g., by the Philistines of Biblical times).
31. Yarmuti and Ibla: regions along the Syrian-Lebanese coast of the
Mediterranean.

Introduction to A Lamentation on the Invasion of Sumer

The invasion of Sumer described in the following composition was
a part of the general catastrophe which brought to an end the dynasty founded by Sargon. For nearly a century thereafter (*ca.* 2200-
2116 B.C.), the Gutians—tribesmen from the Zagros hills—were the
overlords of Mesopotamia.

The Gutians, though they contributed nothing to Mesopotamian civilization, nevertheless did not destroy it. After the first destructiveness of the invasion, they settled down in the cities and began to assimilate something of the civilization of their subjects. Before long, they were dedicating offerings to the Sumerian gods; and they permitted Sumerian cities to be governed by native rulers. We know that in at least one such city—Lagash—Sumerian art, letters, and commerce flourished during the Gutian period.

A LAMENTATION ON THE INVASION OF SUMER BY THE PEOPLE OF GUTIUM

. . . the city, which has been seized . . . , has been annihilated with calamity.

As for . . . mushda,[1] his beloved abode the foot of a stranger inhabits.

His spouse *Nam* . . .

. . . *šagga*[1] wails *repeatedly*.

How long my destroyed habitations, my destroyed temple—shall their misery be?   5

The canal which rejoices the hearts of the cattle waters the fields no more.

The "Canal of Enki,"[2] like a malediction by a curse, is brought to nought.

In the fields rain is not; the land is watered not.

The garden cellars are become heated like an oven and its stores are scattered.

The domestic animals as many as are four-footed of the . . . not.   10

The four-footed animals of the plains repose not.

The god, Lugal-?-da-ge, from his city has been taken away.

As for Ninzu-anna,[3] her beloved abode the foot of the stranger entered.

From *Sumerian Liturgical Texts*, Stephen Langdon, ed., Philadelphia: University of Pennsylvania Museum, 1917, pp. 121-4. Reprinted by permission of the University Museum.
   1. Unidentified deity.
   2. Enki (Ea): god of water and wisdom, patron of the city of Eridu.
   3. A goddess.

How long of her destroyed habitations and her destroyed temple
     shall the misery be?

In Isin[4] mercy and salvation are not: . . . ?   15

The Lady of Isin, princess of the Land,[5] weeps bitterly.

How long of her destroyed habitations and her destroyed temple
     shall the misery be?

[*All of Nippur*],[6] the binder of heaven and earth, by the death
     dealing weapon is smitten.

[Before Enlil,[7]] in this city Nippur a deluge was sent.

Mother Ninlil,[8] mistress of Kiurra,[9] weeps sorrowfully.   20

How long of her destroyed habitations and her destroyed temple
     shall the misery be.

Keš[10] which is built on the plain he has razed like the winds.

In Adab[11] the temple placed by the new canal . . . ?

Hostile Gutium made there his resting place; the stranger
     wreaked destruction.

Gutium rebelled in his heart and exalted his race.   25

Nintud[12] because of his deeds weeps bitterly.

How long of her destroyed habitations and her destroyed temple
     shall the misery be?

. . . in the holy plain he has razed like the wind.

. . . of Innini[13] is plundered and cursed.

Eanna,[14] abode of the "Dark Chamber," the foe beheld.   30

Of the holy "Dark Chamber" the priestly rites are suspended.

. . . from the "Dark Chamber" has been plundered.

. . . the foe carried away.

How long of her destroyed habitations and her destroyed temple
     shall the misery be?

[In Erech?][15] its . . . is seized, light in darkness is overwhelmed.   35

4. A city of central Sumer.
5. Patron goddess of the city.
6. A city on the boundary between the lands of Sumer and Akkad.
7. God of thunder, chief executive of the Sumerian pantheon.
8. A goddess.
9. A region within Sumer; exact location unknown.
10. (Kesh): a city of Sumer, not to be confused with Kish.
11. A city of northern Sumer.
12. (Ninkhursag): a mother-goddess.
13. (Inanna): a love-goddess.
14. The main temple of the city of Uruk in southern Sumer.
15. Erech = Uruk.

Introduction to Gudea, King of Lagash

Lagash is the only city-state whose history we are able to reconstruct in any detail for the period of Gutian suzerainty over Mesopotamia. The city evidently played a leading role in Sumer at this time; but its prominence was economic and cultural, rather than military, in nature. Surviving records from Gudea's reign (*ca.* 2150 B.C.) speak of commerce and temple building rather than of military operations, which evidently were the prerogative of the Gutians. The trade routes to far places were as open as in Sargon's day. Lagash under Gudea enjoyed peace, prosperity, and a great flowering of arts and letters. Although Akkadian influences were already discernible (and would soon thereafter become dominant in Mesopotamian culture), the age of Gudea is generally regarded as embodying the best features of classical Sumerian civilization.

GUDEA, KING OF LAGASH

I

Gudea, *patesi*[1] of Lagash,[2] who Eninnu[3] for Ningirsu[4] built. For Ninkhursag,[5] the lady who causes growth in the city, the mother of its children, his lady, Gudea, *patesi* of Lagash, her temple which is in Girsu[6] built, her holy tablet-receptacle he made; the exalted throne of her ladyship he made, into her exalted temple he brought her. From the mountain of Magan,[7]

Statue inscriptions from *Royal Inscriptions of Sumer and Akkad*, G. A. Barton, ed. and trans., New Haven: Yale University Press, 1929, pp. 181-9. Reprinted by permission of Yale University Press.
1. An old reading of the sign for *ensi* (governor).
2. Lagash was the name both of a city in southern Sumer and the city-state around it. In Gudea's day, Girsu was the capital of the state of Lagash.
3. Temple of the god Ningirsu.
4. Patron deity of the state of Lagash.
5. Also called Nintu (Nintud); a mother-goddess.
6. Capital of the state of Lagash.
7. In this period, the last boundary of the known world, regarded as somewhere to the east, perhaps India.

diorite stone he brought, into his statue he made. "O-lady-who-in-heaven-and-on-earth-fixes-fate-Nintud[8]-mother-of-the-gods-Gudea-who-has-built-the-temple-his-life-prolong!"—with this name he named it and brought it into the temple.

II

In the temple of Ningirsu, his king, the statue of Gudea, *patesi* of Lagash, who Eninnu built. Sixty *qa*[9] of beer; 60 *qa* of food, 10 *qa* of flour, 10 *qa* [of] ground barley, as a perpetual sacrifice he appointed. Should a *patesi* this arrangement overthrow, (or) the decree of Ningirsu hinder, his offering, from the temple of Ningirsu desecrated, may they throw out! may his cries be suppressed! To Ningirsu, the mighty warrior of Enlil,[10] Gudea of established fame, *patesi* of Lagash, the shepherd whose heart was illumined by Ningirsu, whose uplifted eyes were given sight by Nina, whose hand was grasped by Nindar, whose word was inspired by Bau, the child brought forth by Gatumdug, invested with the lordship of the exalted sceptre by Galalim, preserved as a creature of powerful life by Dunshagga, exalted as the leader of all men by Ningishzida,[11] his god, when Ningirsu looked upon his city with his brilliant eyes, Gudea for a faithful shepherd he announced to the land, in the hearts of 216,000 men he established his power; he purified the city, he exalted it. A mould he set up, twin bricks he moulded, a diviner he brought out, a decider, a brilliant male and female searcher of secrets he brought out from the city; his carrying-basket that no woman could lift, the warrior put on his head; the temple of Ningirsu like Eridu[12] a pure place he made; the scourge did not strike, with hand-cuffs no one was oppressed, a mother inflicted no punishment on her child, the eunuch, the overseer, the scribe, the good man stopped work, the fullers of wool ceased the toil of their hands. Among the graves of the city no pick was lifted, no corpse was buried. The priest appointed no dirge; no

8. Nintud = Ninkhursag.
9. A solid measure of about a quart.
10. In Sumerian mythology, chief executive of the gods.
11. Nina . . . Ningishzida = various Sumerian deities.
12. The southernmost city of Sumer.

tear flowed; the wailing woman uttered no lament. Within the boundary of Lagash no litigant on oath put a man, no collector entered into a man's house. For Ningirsu, their king, they joyfully brought their work as a gift, the temple Eninnu of the brilliant black storm-bird they built, its place restored, in it the reed-dwelling which he loved with aromatic cedar they built for him. When the house of Ningirsu he had built, Ningirsu, the king whom he loves, from the upper sea to the lower sea[13] opened his way like a door. From Amanus, the mountain of cedar,[14] cedar trees whose length was 60 cubits,[15] cedar trees whose length was 50 cubits, *ukarinu* trees whose length was 25 cubits, he made into logs and brought down from that mountain. Great beams for battling with the storms he made, great sockets (?) made of bronze, with seven eyes, he made; of worked bronze hand cups for drinking (?) he made; of wrought bronze a laver (?) he made; that cedar wood into great doors he made, with metal stars he beautified them, in Eninnu he set them up. In Emakh,[16] which had been brought low, logs as beams he placed. From the city Ursu on the mountain Ibla[17] *sapalu*-wood, great *amalu*-trees, *tulubu*-trees of the wooded mountain, into logs he made, in Eninnu for beams he placed. From Umalu, a mountain of Menua,[18] from Masalla, a mountain of Amurru,[19] large, long stones he brought down, into *massebahs*[20] he made, on the terrace of Eninnu he set them up. From Tidal, a mountain of Amurru, a large piece of marble he brought, to a high polish he brought it, as its chief ornament (?) in the temple he placed it. From Kagalad, a mountain of Kimash,[21] copper he quarried, into a scepter-head that could

13. Upper and lower seas: the Mediterranean and the Persian Gulf.
14. Region near the Mediterranean coast south of the Gulf of Alexandretta (southernmost Turkey). The Mesopotamians often used the singular term "mountain" to indicate an entire mountainous area.
15. About 18-22 inches, the length of the arm from the end of the middle finger to the elbow.
16. A temple.
17. Near the Mediterranean coast of Syria.
18. A region in Syria.
19. Or Amor: a region of northern Syria west of the Euphrates; also an ethnic group speaking a Semitic language related to Akkadian.
20. An engraved stone or statue.
21. A mountainous region northeast of Assyria.

not be wielded he made it. From the mountain of Melukha[22] he brought down *ushu*-wood, he placed it (in the temple). A piece of *nini*-plant he brought down, into a scepter carved with three lions he made it. Gold-dust from mount Khakhu[23] he brought down, for the sceptre with three lions he appointed it. Gold dust from the mountain of Melukha he brought down, into the body of a chariot he put, (for) a (golden) cow (?) he brought it down. From Gubin,[24] a mountain of *khalupu*-wood, *khalupu*-wood he brought down, into a bird-box cover (cherubim?) he made it. From Madga, a mountain of the river Luruad,[25] asphalt (?) from the banks he brought down, and for the building of the foundations of Eninnu he appointed. A mass of gravel he brought down. From the mountain of Barsip[26] *nalua*-stone on great boats he loaded, the foundations of Eninnu he made strong. The city of Anshan in Elam[27] with weapons he crushed, its booty for Ningirsu to Eninnu he brought; Gudea, *patesi* of Lagash, when Eninnu for Ningirsu had built, with ornamentation he covered it, like a luxurious house he fashioned it, no *patesi* for Ningirsu had so done, or built it, he inscribed his name on it; as an acceptable possession he presented it. The command of Ningirsu his right hand performed. From the mountain of Magan diorite-stone he brought down, into his statues he carved it. "O-my-king-whose-temple-I-have built-let-life-be-my-reward,"—as its name he named it, into Eninnu he carried it. Gudea, the statue a word he spoke: "may the statue (to) my king speak!" When Eninnu, the temple which he loves, he had built, he lifted up his heart, he washed his hands, for seven days grain was not ground; the slave girl walked like her mistress, his slave walked by the side of his king; in my city strong and weak slept side by side. Goods the thief to their house returned. Upon the faithful commands of Nina[28] and Ningirsu verily he fixed his eyes. The poor the rich

22. Often mentioned in connection with Magan: regions to the east of Mesopotamia regarded as distant and exotic.
23. Location unknown.
24. Location unknown.
25. Location uncertain.
26. Borsippa, a city of Akkad, south of Babylon.
27. Mountainous region east of the Tigris, now in southwest Iran.
28. A goddess of vegetation.

man did not oppress. The strong man did not oppress the widow. The house that had no male child its daughter her burning oil brought in, the statue—before it she consumed it. The statue is neither of silver nor of lapis lazuli, nor of bronze, nor of lead nor of copper did a man skilled in tools fashion it; it is of diorite. By a drinking-fountain verily it stands; by the crushing power of his right hand let no man destroy it, while the statue is before thee, O Ningirsu. The statue of Gudea, *patesi* of Lagash, who Eninnu for Ningirsu built, whoever from Eninnu brings it, or its inscription covers over, whoever erases it, (or) at the beginning of a new year, whoever like my god his god Ningirsu, my king, to the people proclaims, (and) my decision alters, my gift removes, from the chant my section (and) my name takes away, (and) his name inserts, in the court of Ningirsu, my king, his offering slays, before whose eyes the fact is not, that from former days, from the beginning, (if) a *patesi* of Lagash Eninnu for Ningirsu, my king, built, whoever an ancient glorious object discovered, no one destroyed it, its decree he did not alter. Gudea, *patesi* of Lagash,—whoever his word breaks, his judgment changes, may Anu,[29] Enlil, Ninkhursag, Enki,[30] whose word is true, Enzu,[31] whose name no one explains, Ningirsu, king of weapons, Nina, lady of abundant vegetation, Nindara, the warlike king, the mother of Lagash, the holy Gatumdug, Bau, the lady, the firstborn of Anu, Ininni, lady of battle, Utu, his king who appointed him, Pa-sag, overseer of the country, Galalim, Dunshaggana, Ninmar, the firstborn child of Nina, Dumuzi of the abyss, the lady of Kinunir, (and) my god, Ningishzida,[32] make his fate destructive, like an ox his days crush, like a wild-ox his terrible strength destroy, the throne which he has established, cast down to the dust, his writing (and) his name cover over, his intelligence take away, his name from the temple of his god from the tablet destroy, his god not look upon the people, the rain of heaven turn away, the water turn from the earth; without a name may he go forth, his reign as a grain-jar

29. Chief of the Sumerian pantheon, a sky-god and patron of Uruk.
30. (Ea): the god of water and wisdom, patron of the city of Eridu.
31. A god, the son of Enlil.
32. Nina . . . Ningishzida = various Sumerian deities.

be cast down. That man like men who do violence to a righteous man, may his corpse unburied be cast down by the city wall, may it be cut in pieces! By the execution of the command of his god, by the lord Ningirsu, his majesty may the people know.

Introduction to Date List
of the Kings of the First Dynasty of Babylon

The following document illustrates a type of historiography which was practiced in Babylonia from the time of Sargon onward. Each year was named after an event that had happened in the preceding year; lists of such names were kept in order to maintain their correct sequence. The usefulness of these lists to the modern historian is somewhat restricted by their formalism and limited scope: they mention chiefly pious acts, wars, and building projects. Nonetheless, such lists preserve for us the outline of over five hundred years of Babylonian history.

The text of the following, from the reigns of Hammurabi, king of Babylon from 1792 to 1750 B.C., and his son Samsu-iluna (1749-1712 B.C.), is badly broken.

DATE LIST OF THE KINGS OF THE FIRST DYNASTY OF BABYLON

Reign of Hammurabi

The year of Hammurabi, the king.
The year in which righteousness was established in the land.
The year in which the throne of the exalted shrine of Nannar[1] was made in Babylon.

From *Chronicles Concerning Early Babylonian Kings*, L. W. King, ed. and trans., London: Luzac and Company, 1907, pp. 97-102 and 103-5. Reprinted by permission.
1. (Nanna): the moon-god.

The year in which the wall of Malgia[2] was built.

The year in which the . . . of the god was made.   5

The year in which the fortress of the goddess Laz (was built).

The year in which the [wall] of Isin[3] (was . . .).

The year in which . . . the land of Emutbal[4] . . . .

The year in which the Hammurabi-khegallu Canal (was dug).

The year in which the inhabitants and the cattle of Malgia
     (were carried off).   10

The year in which the cities of Rabiku and Shalibi[5] (were
     captured).

The year in which the throne of Sarpanitum[6] (was made).

The year in which the king entered Umu-ki[7] and great abun-
     dance (was established).

The year in which the throne of Ishtar[8] of Babylon (was made).

The year in which his (i.e., Hammurabi's) seven images (were
     made).   15

The year in which the throne of Nabu[9] (was made).

The year in which the images of Ishtar and Adad[10]. . . .

The year in which the exalted lady of Bel[11]. . . .

The year in which the fortress of Igi-kharsagga[12] (was built).

The year in which the throne of Adad (was made).   20

The year in which the wall of the city of Basu[13] (was. . .) .

The year in which the image of Hammurabi, the king of
     righteousness, (was made).

The year in which the . . . of the city of Sippar[14] (was . . .).

The year in which . . . for Bel (was made).

2. Region to the east of Sumer across the Tigris.

3. A city of central Sumer, former seat of a dynasty.

4. A waterway, the boundary of a region east of the Tigris.

5. Rabiku is located on the Euphrates, Shalibi presumably somewhere nearby.

6. A goddess, the spouse of Marduk.

7. Current scholarship believes this word to indicate a kind of metal, per- haps copper. Thus the translation of this line is misleading.

8. Goddess of love.

9. (Nebo): a god of the city of Borsippa.

10. Adad: the god of storm and rain.

11. Bel: another name for Marduk, chief of the gods of Babylonia.

12. A small settlement near Babylon.

13. (Bazi): a town northwest of Babylon, later the seat of a dynasty.

14. A city in Akkad.

The year in which the wall of the city of Sippar (was built).   25

(The text is missing for the 26th through the 39th year of Hammurabi's reign.)

The year in which. . . .   40
The year in which. . . .
The year in which the wall of the city of . . . (was . . .).
The year in which the dust of the cities of Sippar and Ul-
    Shamash[15]. . . .
The forty-three years of Hammurabi, the king.

Reign of Samsu-iluna

The year of Samsu-iluna, the king, in which his dominion over
    the world . . . was established.
The year in which the independence of Sumer [and Akkad was
    established].
The year in which the canal named Samsu-iluna-nagab-nuk-
    hush-nishi was dug.
The year in which the canal named Samsu-iluna-khegallu was
    dug.
The year in which the throne of the shrine of Nannar and Sag-
    du-gud[16] (was made).   5
The year in which the image . . . of the god . . . (was made).
The year in which the masrakhu[17] (was made).
The year in which the king entered Umu-ki,[7] and mountain and
    river alike (gave abundance).
The year in which the army of the Kassites[18]. . . .
The year in which the army. . . .   10
The year in which the wall(s) of the cities of Ur and Erech[19]
    (were built).
The year in which the land of Amsia[20]. . . .

(The text is missing for the remaining years of Samsu-iluna.)

15. Ul-Shamash: probably should be, "Sippar, the city of Shamash. . . ."
16. Sag-du-gud: epithet for the god Nanna.
17. A standard (banner).
18. Their location at this period has not been established.
19. Cities of southern and central Sumer.
20. An enemy. Probably should read "land of *the* Amsia."

Introduction to The Lamentation over the Destruction of Ur

During the period of Gutian overlordship, the city of Ur was ruled by governors (*ensi*'s) who sometimes acknowledged the supremacy of the rulers of Lagash or Uruk. The founder of the famous Third Dynasty of Ur was one Ur-Nammu, once a general of Utuhengal, that king of Uruk who expelled the Gutians from Mesopotamia (*ca.* 2112 B.C.) and ended their political influence over the lowlands forever. Shortly after Utuhengal's victory, Ur-Nammu overthrew his chief, established himself in Ur, and proceeded to create an empire.

The Third Dynasty of Ur (*ca.* 2112-2004 B.C.) marks one of the outstanding periods of Mesopotamian history. The empire of Ur included Sumer, Akkad, and northern Mesopotamia as far as Mari on the Upper Euphrates and Ashur in Assyria. A lucrative commerce flourished. We hear of land surveys, an extensive building program, and efficient administration of the empire by temple scribes. Ur-Nammu also promulgated laws, of which some fragments have survived. The Third Dynasty of Ur maintained a stability and unity in the land unequaled before that time.

This flourishing empire gradually disintegrated under the pressures of the particularism of various cities and the continual influx of Semitic nomads from the borderlands. The cities of northern Mesopotamia lost contact with the capital and drifted apart from the empire. The death blow came at the hands of the Elamites from the eastern hills, who overran Sumer and carried off the last king of the Third Dynasty, Ibbi-Sin, to captivity in Elam (*ca.* 2004 B.C.). The ruins of the city of Ur testify to the savagery with which the Elamites revenged themselves upon their former overlord. The great buildings constructed under the Third Dynasty were destroyed, the temples plundered of their treasures. At the same time, Amorite tribes led by the ruler of Mari occupied the land of Akkad.

This disaster marks the end of Sumerian political leadership in Mesopotamia. The territories of the Third Dynasty broke apart into city-states, such as Isin and Larsa; and the empires to follow in Mesopotamia, down to the Persian conquest, were dominated by

Semites. But Sumerian civilization did not die. During this period of political decline, many of the great works of Sumerian literature were written down. The Akkadians and the Assyrians preserved Sumerian as a sacred language and adapted its script to their own quite different tongues.

Commemorating the destruction of Ur, the following poem was probably both composed and inscribed during the so-called early post-Sumerian period (comprising the dynasties of Isin, Larsa, and Babylon I). While it cannot be dated precisely, analyses of its grammar and orthography show it to be considerably later than "classical" Sumerian. It is almost unique among extant Sumerian literary works in that an almost complete text can be pieced together from surviving fragments. Numerous variants of the work have been excavated—mostly at Nippur—making possible a nearly complete restoration.

The lamentation consists of 436 lines, arranged into eleven groups or "songs" of uneven length which are separated by the antiphons following each song. It exhibits several characteristics typical of Sumerian poetry: the use of parallelism, frequent repetition of a single phrase, and the arrangement into couplets in which the second line repeats the contents of the first, word for word, except that the person, deity, place, etc. which was only hinted at in the first line is now actually named. The composition was meant to be recited or chanted to the accompaniment of musical instruments, though we can only guess as to the occasion on which this occurred.

The portion of the lamentation here reproduced begins with the plaint of the goddess Ningal before her husband, Nanna, attempting to arouse him to the fate of her city. It goes on to describe a devastating "evil storm" which turned Ur and all of Sumer into ruins, while the "good storm," the "storm of overflow," failed to appear. Apparently the ravages of nature—flood, wind, rain—are meant, for only two of the 32 lines of this fifth song refer to destructive forces other than the elements. But the "storm" of the sixth song is clearly of another kind: the disasters befalling the city as the result of foreign invasion are described. In the seventh song, the goddess once again takes up the lament for her city. The ninth and tenth songs contain pleas to the god Nanna not to permit the city and the "black-headed people" to be overwhelmed entirely by the calamities they have suffered. The final song, which is imperfectly preserved, consists of a prayer to Nanna to restore Ur to its former position of eminence.

THE LAMENTATION OVER THE DESTRUCTION OF UR

2

O city, a bitter lament set up as thy lament;   40
Thy lament which is bitter—O city, set up thy lament.
His righteous city which has been destroyed—bitter is its lament;
His Ur which has been destroyed—bitter is its lament.
Thy lament which is bitter—O city, set up thy lament;
His Ur which has been destroyed—bitter is its lament.   45
Thy lament which is bitter—how long will it grieve thy weeping lord?
Thy lament which is bitter—how long will it grieve the weeping Nanna?[1]

. . . .

O thou city *of name*, thou hast been destroyed;   65
O thou city *of high walls*, thy land has perished.
O my city, like an innocent ewe thy lamb has been torn away from thee;
O Ur, like an innocent goat thy kid has perished.
O city, thy *parsû*,[2] the dread and awe of the enemy,
Thy decrees—unto inimical decrees they have been transformed.   70
Thy lament which is bitter—how long will it grieve thy weeping lord?
Thy lament which is bitter—how long will it grieve the weeping Nanna?

The second song.

From *Lamentation Over the Destruction of Ur*, S. N. Kramer, ed. ("Assyriological Studies," No. 12, Oriental Institute), Chicago: University of Chicago Press, 1940. Copyright 1940 by the University of Chicago. Reprinted by permission.
  1. The moon-god (also known as Sin). He and his wife Ningal were worshipped especially at Ur.
  2. A word with no exact equivalent in English. It indicates the character of a city, god, people, etc., or that which determines or regulates its characteristics.

His [righteous city] which [has been destroyed]—bitter is its
　　lament;
His Ur which has been destroyed—bitter is its lament.   75
Its antiphon.

4

"On that day, after *the lord had been overcome by the storm,*
After, *in spite of the 'lady,'*[3] her city had been destroyed;
On that day, after *the lord had been overwhelmed by the storm,*
After they had *commanded* the utter destruction of my[4] city;   140
After they had *commanded* the utter destruction of Ur,
After they had ordered that its people be killed—
On that day verily I abandoned not my city;
My land verily I forsake not.
To Anu[5] the water of my eye verily I poured;   145
To Enlil[6] I in person verily made supplication.
'Let not my city be destroyed,' verily I said unto them;
'Let not Ur be destroyed,' verily I said unto them;
'Let not its people perish,' verily I said unto them.
Verily Anu turned not to this word;   150
Verily Enlil with its 'It is good; so be it' soothed not my heart.
For the second time, when the council had . . .-ed
(And) the Anunnaki[7] . . . *had seated themselves,*
The *legs* verily I . . .-ed, the arms verily I *stretched out.*
To Anu the water of my eye verily I poured;   155
To Enlil I in person verily made supplication.
'Let not my city be destroyed,' verily I said unto them;
'Let not Ur be destroyed,' verily I said unto them;
'Let not its people perish,' verily I said unto them.
Verily Anu turned not to this word;   160
Verily Enlil with its 'It is good; so be it' soothed not my heart.
The utter destruction of my city verily they ordered,

3. "Lord" and "lady" refer to Nanna and Ningal, the patron deities of Ur.
4. The goddess Ningal is speaking.
5. Chief god of the Sumerian pantheon, a sky-god and patron of the city
of Uruk (Erech).
6. The god of thunder, who brought abundance and prosperity, but was
also capable of destructiveness.
7. The judges of the underworld.

The utter destruction of Ur verily they ordered;
That its people be killed, as its fate verily they decreed.
Me like one who had given them my . . .   165
Me *because of* my city they *filled* with *grief*;
My Ur *because of* me they *filled* with *grief*.
Anu changes not his command;
Enlil alters not the command which he had issued."

The fourth song.   170
Her city has been destroyed; her decrees have become inimical.
Its antiphon.

5

Enlil called to the storm,   The people groan.
The storm of overflow he carried off from
      the land;   The people groan.
The good storm he carried off from Sumer.   The people groan.   175
To the evil storm he gave (his) order;   The people groan.
The great work set aside for each storm he gave into his hand.
To the storm that annihilates the land he
      called;   The people groan.
To all the evil winds he called.   The people groan.
Enlil brings Gibil[8] to his aid;   180
To the great storm of heaven he called.   The people groan.
The great storm howls above;   The people groan.
The land-annihilating storm roars below.   The people groan.
The evil wind like the rushing torrent cannot be restrained;
The boats of the city it attacks (and) *devours*.   185
At the base of heaven *it made the* . . .
      whirl,   The people groan.
In front of the storm *it made fire burn*;   The people groan.
At the side of the battling storms it *intensified* the tumult,
In the rain-bearing . . . *of the day it made fire burn*.
The bright light sent forth by the day, the good light, it with-
      held;   190
In the land it sent not forth bright light, like *a twilight star
      it shone*.

8. The fire-god.

The night during the celebration of its feasts and banquets was
    overwhelmed by the South Wind;
At the side of their cups dust was piled
    high;   The people groan.
Over the black-headed people the winds
    swept.   The people groan.
Sumer *is broken up by* the *gišburru;*[9]   The people groan.   195
Upon the land it makes . . . (and) *devours* it.
The afflicting storm by tears is not adjured;
The destructive storm makes the land tremble and quake,
Like the storm of the flood it destroys the cities.
The land-annihilating storm set up (its) decrees in the city;   200
The all-destroying storm came doing evil;
Like a . . . it *placed* the . . . upon the people.
The evil, afflicting storm, the command of Enlil, the storm un-
    ceasingly undermining the land
Covered Ur like a garment, *enveloped* it like linen.

The fifth song.   205
The raging storm has attacked unceasingly.   The people groan.
Its antiphon.

6

On that day the (good) storm was carried off from the city; that
    city into ruins,
O Father Nanna, that city into ruins was
    made.   The people groan.
On that day the (good) storm was carried
    off from the land;   The people groan.   210
Its people *without a potsherd filled its sides;*
On its walls *they lay prostrate.*   The people groan.
In its lofty gates where they were wont to promenade dead
    bodies were lying about;
In its boulevards where the feasts were celebrated they were
    viciously attacked.

---

9. A club-like weapon used in battle or for ceremonial purposes. Or: a
trap used in hunting.

In all its streets where they were wont to promenade dead
    bodies were lying about;   215
In its places where the festivities of the land took place the
    people were *ruthlessly laid low.*
The blood of the land like bronze and lead . . . ;
Its dead bodies, like fat put to the flame, of themselves melted
    away.
Its men who were brought to an end by the ax did not cover
    themselves with the *helmet;*
Like a gazelle held fast by the *gišburru,*[9] (their) mouths bit the
    dust.   220
Its men who were struck down by the *spear* did not fasten about
    them the . . . ;
*Lo, (as) in the place where their mother labored they lay
    stricken in their blood.*
Its men who were brought to an end by the *battle mace* did not
    fasten about them the . . . ;
Like men who cannot drink strong drink, they drooped neck
    over shoulder.
Who was stationed near the weapons by the
    weapons was killed;   The people groan.   225
Who escaped them by the storm was
    prostrated.   The people groan.
Ur—its weak and (its) strong perished through hunger;
Mothers and fathers who did not leave (their) houses were
    overcome by fire;
The young lying on their mothers' bosoms like fish were carried
    off by the waters;
The nursing mothers—pried open were their breasts.   230
The judgment of the land perished;   The people groan.
The counsel of the land *was dissipated.*   The people groan.
The mother left her daughter;   The people groan.
The father turned away from his son.   The people groan.
In the city the wife was abandoned, the child was abandoned,
    the possessions were scattered about;   235
The black-headed people *wherever they laid their heads . . .
    were carried off.*
Its lady like a flying bird departed from her city;

Ningal like a flying bird departed from her city.
On all its possessions which had been accumulated in the land a
    defiling hand was placed.
In all its *storehouses* which abounded in the land fires were
    kindled;   240
At its rivers Gibil, the purified, relentlessly did (his) work.
The lofty unapproachable mountain, the Ekišširgal[10]—
Its righteous house by large axes *is devoured*;
The Sutians[11] and the Elamites,[12] the destroyers, *made (of) it
    thirty shekels.*
The righteous house they *break up* with the
    pickax;   The people groan.   245
The city they make into ruins.   The people groan.
Its lady cries: "Alas for my city," cries: "Alas for my house";
Ningal cries: "Alas for my city," cries: "Alas for my house.
As for me, the lady, my city has been destroyed, my house too
    has been destroyed;
O Nanna, Ur has been destroyed, its people have been dis-
    persed."   250

The sixth song.
In her stable, in her sheepfold the lady utters bitter words:
    "The city is being destroyed by the storm."
Its antiphon.

7

Mother Ningal in her city like an enemy stood aside.
The lady loudly utters there the wail for her attacked house;   255
The princess in Ur, her attacked shrine, bitterly cries:
"Verily Anu has cursed my city, my city verily has been de-
    stroyed;
Verily Enlil has turned inimical to my house, by the *pickax*
    verily it has been *torn up*.
Upon him who comes from below verily he hurled fire—alas,
    my city verily has been destroyed;

---

10. The shrine where Nanna and Ningal were worshipped.
11· Or Su-people, from the desert region west of Mesopotamia.
12. Peoples from the eastern borderlands, today southwestern Iran.

Enlil upon him who comes from above verily hurled the flame.   260
Outside the city, the outside of the city verily has been destroyed
   —'alas for my city' I will say;
Inside the city, the inside of the city verily has been destroyed—
   'alas for my house' I will say.
My houses of the outside of the city verily have been de-
   stroyed—'alas for my city' I will say;
My houses of the inside of the city verily have been destroyed—
   'alas for my house' I will say.
My city like an innocent ewe has not been . . .-ed, gone is its
   trustworthy shepherd;   265
Ur like an innocent ewe has not been . . .-ed, gone is its shepherd
   boy.
My ox in its stable has not been . . .-ed, gone is its herdsman;
My sheep in its fold has not been . . .-ed, gone is its shepherd
   boy.
In the rivers of my city dust has gathered, into . . . verily they
   have been made;
In their midst no sparkling waters flow, gone is its *river-worker*.   270
In the fields of the city there is no grain, gone is its fieldworker;
My fields verily like fields *torn up* by the *pickax* have brought
   forth . . .
My palm groves and vineyards that abounded with honey and
   wine verily have brought forth the mountain thorn;
My plain where *kazallu*[13] *and* strong drink were prepared verily
   like *an oven* has become *parched*.
My possessions like *heavy locusts* on the move verily . . . *have
   been carried off*—'O my possessions' I will say;   275
My possessions verily he who came from the lower lands to the
   lower lands has carried off—'O my possessions' I will say;
My possessions verily he who came from the upper lands to the
   upper lands has carried off—'O my possessions' I will say.
Verily my (precious) metal, stone, and lapis lazuli have been
   scattered about—'O my possessions' I will say;
My treasure verily . . . has been dissipated—'O my possessions'
   I will say.

13. A plant used for medicinal purposes.

My (precious) metal verily they who know not (precious) metal have fastened about their hands;   28(

My (precious) stone verily they who know not (precious) stone have fastened about their necks.

Verily all my birds and *winged creatures* have flown away— 'alas for my city' I will say;

My daughters and sons verily . . . have been carried off—'alas for my men' I will say.

Woe is me, my daughters verily in a strange city carry strange banners;

With . . . verily *the young men and young women have been fastened.*   28(

[*Woe is me*, my city] which no longer exists—I am not its queen;

[O Nanna,] Ur which no longer exists—I am not its mistress.

I whose house verily has been made *into ruins*, whose city verily has been destroyed,

I, the righteous lady, in place of whose city verily strange cit*ie*s ha*v*e been built,

I whose city verily has been made *into ruins*, whose house verily has been destroyed,   29(

I, Ningal, in place of whose house verily strange houses ha*v*e been built—

Woe is me, the city has been destroyed, the house too has been destroyed;

O Nanna, the shrine Ur has been destroyed, its people are dead."

9

Alas, all the storms together have flooded the land.

The great storm of heaven, the ever roaring storm,

Which sated the land with affliction;   39(

The storm which destroys cities, the storm which destroys houses;

The storm which destroys stables, the storm which destroys sheepfolds;

Which stretched out (its) hand over the holy *parsû*,[14]

Which placed a defiling hand on the weighty counsel;

14. See note 2 above.

Which cut off the light of the land, *the good,*   395
Which banned the light of the black-headed people. (*Alas,* all
    the storms together have flooded the land.)

The ninth song.
The storm which . . .
Its antiphon.

10

The storm which knows not the mother, the storm which knows
    not the father,   400
The storm which knows not the wife, the storm which knows
    not the child,
The storm which knows not the sister, the storm which knows
    not the brother,
The storm which knows not the weak, the storm which knows
    not the strong,
The storm on whose account the wife is forsaken, on whose ac-
    count the child is forsaken,
The storm which caused the light to perish in the land,   405
Which sated it with evil and affliction—
O Father Nanna, let not that storm establish itself *near* thy city!
Let it not cast down thy black-headed people *before thee!*
Let not that storm like rain pouring down from heaven
    turn . . . !
(The storm) which *overwhelmed* the living creatures of heaven
    and earth, the black-headed people—   410
May that storm be entirely destroyed!
Like the great gate of night may the door be closed on it!
Let not that storm be given a place in the *numbering!*
May its record *hang by a nail outside* the house of Enlil!

The tenth song.   415
Unto distant days, other days, future days.
Its antiphon.

11

From distant days, when the land was founded,
O Nanna, the . . . *who have taken thy path*

Have brought unto thee *their* tears *of the smitten* house; before
  thee *is their cry!*   42

May thy black-headed people who have been cast away
  prostrate themselves unto thee!

May thy city which has been made into ruins set up a wail unto
  thee!

O Nanna, may thy city which has been returned to its place step
  forth gloriously before thee!

Like a bright star let it not be destroyed; may it proceed before
  thee!

. . . man shall . . . ;   42

[*The man*] of [offer]ings shall utter prayers unto thee.

. . . who art . . . of the [lan]d,

. . . . ,

Undo the sins of its . . . !

May the heart of its . . . be soothed!   43

Upon its man of offerings, *who is standing*, gaze with steadfast
  eye!

O Nanna, thou whose penetrating gaze *overwhelms* every heart,

May every evil heart of its people be pure before thee!

May the hearts of those who dwell in the land be *good* before
  thee!

O Nanna, thy city which has been returned to its place exalts
  thee.   43

The eleventh song.

Introduction to The Gilgamesh Epic

The Gilgamesh epic is the longest Babylonian poem yet discovered,
and the principal surviving epic from before the time of Homer.
Probably it was composed about 2000 B.C., though it is possible
that certain elements were added later. However, the prominence
assigned in the epic to the old Sumerian chief deities Anu and
Enlil and the complete omission of Marduk, the principal god in
Hammurabi's day, indicates that the poem must antedate the First

Dynasty of Babylon. Many of its episodes are undoubtedly even older; for some of them have been found as separate tales on Sumerian tablets from the third millennium B.C.; and certainly they existed in oral form long before being put into writing. The epic proper comes to a logical end with Tablet XI, concluding with almost the same words with which the poem begins, indicating that the cycle of myths and legends of Gilgamesh is thereby completed.

Gilgamesh may originally have been a historical personage. The semi-historical list of Sumerian kings records a ruler of that name, the fifth in line after the Flood to rule in Uruk (Erech), who is said to have reigned for 126 years. Among others of this First Dynasty of Uruk were the gods Dumuzi and Lugalbanda, who, like Gilgamesh, enjoyed reigns of superhuman length and may also have been real kings before they became gods. In any event, to the Sumerians of 2000 B.C., the First Dynasty lay far back in the dim mists of history. It was easy for myths and legends to attach themselves to the names of these early rulers: Gilgamesh himself eventually became a king of the underworld.

The epic may be considered on several different levels. Most obviously, it is a simple tale of adventure. Gilgamesh and his friend Enkidu are drawn in heroic proportions: their strength and physical prowess are far superior to that of ordinary mortals. Ambitious to acquire a hero's fame, Gilgamesh journeys down to the cedar forest "to establish a name for myself." The giant Huwawa, guardian of the forest, is an opponent of superhuman stature, as is the bull of Heaven, sent by the goddess Ishtar to avenge Gilgamesh's insults to her.

The poem also contains elements of historical truth. Uruk was an actual Sumerian city ruled by real kings who prided themselves upon building great walls and temples, the ruins of which may still be seen. This civilization of the river valleys was surrounded and often threatened by wild tribes from the borderlands. One such barbarian was Gilgamesh's friend Enkidu, born on the steppe, who roamed with the wild animals and shared their food. The poem's description of his strange appearance and uncultured habits doubtless reflects the superiority felt by the civilized city-dweller *vis-à-vis* the barbarian. Enkidu's seduction by a harlot from the city (surely the "wicked" city in barbarian eyes) and his acquisition of citified manners is an allegory of the process by which the border peoples were gradually but steadily brought within the circle of civilization. Enkidu's deathbed curse represents his regret at this loss of innocence.

Gilgamesh's expedition to the cedar forest reflects a fact of Babylonian economic life—the trading journeys necessary for acquiring the timber unavailable in the lowland valleys. No doubt such expeditions were accompanied by many hardships and by the opposition of tribes along the way—dangers personified in the figure of the giant Huwawa, protector of the cedars. The bull of Heaven with its terrible, hot breath represents the drought which ensued whenever the Tigris and Euphrates failed to overflow, bringing their fertile alluvium to cover the land.

The story is also full of supernatural elements, which to the Babylonians no doubt were perfectly credible: the enchanted gate of the forest; Gilgamesh's mysterious sleep; the plant which grants immortality; the descent to the nether world. The intervention of divine powers in human affairs was, indeed, expected; for according to Mesopotamian belief, mankind had been created specifically to serve the gods' very prosaic needs. Events on earth were believed to be the direct result of the gods' decrees: thus the council of the gods discusses Enkidu's offense in slaying the bull of Heaven, and decides that he must die. Thereupon Gilgamesh resolves to cross the ocean (somewhere beyond the Persian Gulf) which was regarded as the boundary of the earth, and which joined the waters of death.

Thus, on a deeper level, the poem is a consideration of the meaning of life. At the outset, Gilgamesh is the naïve hero, two-thirds god and one-third man, rejoicing in his strength and eager to prove his prowess. The death of Enkidu forces him into an awareness of man's existential situation, which not even a hero can escape. Death to the Mesopotamians was the natural consequence of man's constitution, to be followed by the decay of the body and the journey of the spirit to the underworld, where it was doomed to exist forever after in shadowy darkness. Gilgamesh is denied even the hope of resurrection: death means that he will "lie down and not rise forever." Condemned by his humanness to share the common fate of mankind, he becomes a tragic hero. His quest for immortality ends in failure, but even at the end of the poem, he is scarcely resigned to the unavoidable.

Despite its philosophical and religious overtones, the Gilgamesh epic is a secular poem. Unlike *Enuma Elish*, it was not intended for recitation upon any religious occasion. In its present form, it is a Semitic Babylonian compilation of originally unrelated myths and legends, mostly of Sumerian origin. The episodes of the slaying of

Huwawa, the Flood (with its obvious similarities to the Old Testament story), the proposal of Ishtar to Gilgamesh, and the descent of the bull of Heaven all have been discovered as separate tales on Sumerian tablets. Tablet XII of the epic (not reproduced here) is obviously a later addition; for it partially contradicts what precedes. Enkidu's death occurs in Tablet VII; but at the beginning of Tablet XII he is still alive: Gilgamesh sends him to the underworld to recover two lost objects, and there he is prevented from returning. As indicated by the numerous variant versions, the epic was continually modified and elaborated over the centuries.

Forgotten during the classical age of Greece and Rome, the Gilgamesh epic came to light again only in the nineteenth century with the excavation of the ruins of Nineveh, former capital of the Assyrian empire. Ashurbanipal (reigned 668-627 B.C.), the last great king of Assyria, was an enthusiastic collector of antiquities. His palace library contained a notable collection of ancient hymns, poems, and scientific and religious texts, among which was the epic of Gilgamesh. This Assyrian version of the poem consists of twelve large tablets, each containing about three hundred lines, except for the twelfth, which has only about half that number. Since this discovery, numerous other fragments belonging to the cycle of Gilgamesh legends have come to light—from the ruins of Sippar, Uruk, Ashur, Nippur, Kish, Ur, and even a few from the Hittite capital of Hattusas. Nonetheless, portions of some of the tablets are still missing, though the main story has now been reconstructed.

The account of the Flood in the Gilgamesh epic has been of considerable interest to Old Testament scholars. The parallels between the two versions of this event are quite striking; and some connection between them can scarcely be denied. Since the Old Testament version is undoubtedly the later of the two, many scholars consider it to be dependent on the Gilgamesh account. Possibly both drew upon an age-old tradition current in Mesopotamia. In any event, the orientation of the two versions is quite different. The Hebrew story stresses the omnipotence of Yahweh, who sends the Flood, and his ethical demands upon mankind, which must suffer for its sinfulness. In the Gilgamesh epic, the reasons for the Flood are unclear, but apparently due to godly caprice. Though there is an incidental reference to man's sin, we are not told the nature of the offense. The Babylonian account is also polytheistic: the gods quarrel about the wisdom of sending the Flood and subsequently regret their decision. Thus despite a common skeleton and many similar details, the two versions serve quite different purposes and demonstrate widely divergent conceptions of the nature of divinity and the duties of man.

The following translation has been pieced together from the various surviving fragments of the epic.

THE GILGAMESH EPIC

Tablet I/Column i

[He who] saw everything [within the confi]nes(?) of the land;
[He who] knew [all things and was versed(?) in] everything;
[. . .] together [. . .];
[. . .] wisdom, who everything [. . .].
He saw]se[cret thing(s) and [revealed] hidden thing(s);   5
He brought intelligence of (the days) before the flo[od];
He went on a long journey, became weary and [worn];
[He engra]ved on a table of stone all the travail.
He built the wall of Uruk, the enclosure,
Of holy Eanna,[1] the sacred storehouse.   10
Behold its outer wall, whose brightness is like (that of) copper!
Yea, look upon its inner wall, which none can equal!
Take hold of the threshold, which is from of old!
Approach Eanna, the dwelling of Ishtar,
Which no later king, no man, can equal!   15
Climb upon the wall of Uruk (and) walk about;
Inspect the foundation terrace and examine the brickwork,
If its brickwork be not of burnt bricks,
(And if) the seven [wise men] did not lay its foundation![2]

From *The Gilgamesh Epic and Old Testament Parallels*, A. Heidel, ed. and trans., Chicago: University of Chicago Press, 1946, 1949. Copyright 1946, 1949 by the University of Chicago; reprinted by permission. Passages put into Latin by Heidel have been rendered into English with the aid of Professor John Hawthorne of the University of Chicago.

1. Principal sanctuary of the city of Uruk. It was dedicated to Anu, patron deity of Uruk, and to his daughter Ishtar, goddess of love.

2. Compare Tablet XI, lines 304-5 below. In Mesopotamian mythology, seven wise men were the bringers of civilization to the seven oldest cities of the land.

At this point the Assyrian recension, to which we owe virtually all the material on this tablet, breaks off. To judge from the length of the other columns of this tablet, about thirty lines are missing. Some of this material, however, can be restored from the opening passage of the Hittite version, which, after two almost completely destroyed lines, reads as follows:

After Gilgamesh was created(?),
The valiant god [. . . perfected] his form . . .
The heavenly Shamash[3] granted him [comeliness];   5
Adad[4] granted him heroism [. . .].
The form of Gilgamesh the great gods [made surpassing].
Eleven cubits [was his height]; the breadth of his chest was
    nine [spans].
The length of his [. . .] was three(?) [. . .].
[Now] he turns hither and thither [to see] all the lands.   10
To the city of Uruk he comes [. . .].

After a few more fragmentary lines the Hittite text breaks off. The second column of the Assyrian version, setting in before line 10 of the Hittite fragment, continues the description of Gilgamesh.

Tablet I/Column ii

Two-(thirds) of him is god and [one-third of him is man].
The form of his body [none can match (?)].

(Lines 3-8 almost completely destroyed.)

The onslaught of [his] weapons has no [equ]al.
[His] fellows are. . . .   10
The men of Uruk fu[me] in [their] cha[mbers(?)]:
"Gilgamesh lea[ves] no son to [his] fath[er];
[Day] and [night his] outra[geousness] continues
    unrestrained.
[Yet Gilga]mesh [is the shepherd] of Uruk, the enc[losure].
He is [our] shepherd, [strong, handsome, and wise].   15
[Gilgamesh] leaves no [virgin to her lover],
The daughter of a war[rior, the chosen of a noble]!"

3. The sun-god.
4. The god of storm and rain.

Their lament [the gods heard over and over again].
The gods of heaven [called] the Lord of Uruk:[5]
"[Aruru(?)][6] brought this furious wild ox into being.   20
[The onslaught of his weapons] has no equal.
[His fellows] are. . . .
Gilgamesh leaves no son to his father, day and ni[ght his out-
    rageousness continues unrestrained];
And he is the shepherd of Uruk, [the enclosure];
He is their shepherd, and (yet) [he oppresses them(?)].   25
Strong, handsome, (and) wise [. . .].
Gilgamesh leaves no virgin to [her lover],
The daughter of a warrior, the chosen of a no[ble]!"
When [Anu] heard their lament over and over again,
Great Aruru they called: "Thou, Aruru, didst create
    [Gilgamesh(?)];   30
Now create his equal, to the impetuosity of his heart let him be
    eq[ual].
Let them ever strive (with each other), and let Uruk (thus)
    have re[st]."
When Aruru heard this, she conceived in her heart an image of
    Anu;
[A]ruru washed her hands, pinched off clay, (and) threw (it)
    on the steppe:
[. . .] valiant Enkidu she created, the offspring . . . of
    Ninurta.[7]   35
His whole body is [cov]ered with hair, the hair of (his) head
    is like (that of) a woman;
The locks of the hair of his head sprout like grain.
He knows nothing about people or land, he is clad in a garb like
    Sumuqan.[8]
With the gazelles he eats grass;
With the game he presses on to the drinking-place;   40
With the animals his heart delights at the water.

5. The god Anu, who was also the chief god of all Sumer.
6. A goddess.
7. God of war.
8. God of cattle and vegetation.

A hunter, a trapper,
Met him face to face at the drinking-place;
[One] day, a second, and a third (day) he met him face to face
    at the drinking-place.
The hunter saw him, and his face was benumbed with fear;   45
He went into his house with his game,
[He was af]frighted, benumbed, and quiet.
His heart [was stirred], his face was overclouded;
Woe [entered] his heart;
His face was like (that of) [one who had made] a far
    [journey].   50

Tablet I/Column iii

The hunter opened [his mouth] and, addressing [his father],
    said:
"[My] father, there is a [unique] man who has co[me to thy
    field].
He is the [st]rong(est) [on the steppe]; stren[gth he has];
(And) [his strength] is strong [like that of) the host] of
    heaven.
[He ranges at large] over thy field [. . .];   5
[He ever eats grass] with the game;
[He ever sets] his [fo]ot toward the drinking-place.
[I am afraid and] do [not] dare to approach h[im].
[The p]its which I dug [he has filled in again];
The traps which I se[t he has torn up];   10
[He helps] the game (and) animals of the ste[ppe to escape out
    of my hands]
(And) [does not allow] me to catch the game of the steppe.[9]
[His father opened his mouth and,] addressing the hunter,
    [said]:
"[My son, in] Uruk [there lives] Gilgamesh;
[There is no one who] has prevailed against him;   15
His strength is str[ong like (that of) the host of heaven].
[Go, se]t thy face [toward Uruk];
[Tell Gilgamesh of] the strength of (this) man.

    9. Literally, "(He does not allow) me the doing of the steppe."

[Let him give thee a courtesan, a prostitute, and] lead (her)
    [with thee];
[Let the courtesan] like a strong one [prevail against him].   20
[When he waters the game at] the drinking-place,
Let her take off her robe and bare her beauty.
[When he sees h]er, he will approach her.
(But then) his game, [which grew up on] his steppe, will
    change its attitude toward him."
[Listening] to the advice of his father,   25
The hunter went [to Gilgamesh].
He set out on (his) journey (and) st[opped] in Uruk.
[Addressing himself to] Gilga[mesh, he said]:
"There is a unique man who [has come to the field of my
    father].
He is the strong(est) on the steppe; [strength he has];   30
(And) [his strength] is strong like (that of) the host of heaven.
He ranges at large over the field [of my father];
He ever [eats grass] with the game;
He ever [sets] his foot toward the drinking-place.
I am afraid and do not dare to approach [him].   35
The pits which I d[ug] he has filled in (again);
The traps [which I set] he has torn up.
He helps the game (and) animals [of the steppe] to escape out
    of my hands
(And) does not allow me to catch the game of the steppe."
Gilgamesh said to him, [to] the hunter: 40
"Go, my hunter, take with thee a courtesan, a prostitute,
And when he w[aters] the game at the drinking-place,
Let her take off her robe and bare her beauty.
When he sees her, he will approach her.
(But then) his game, which grew up on his steppe, will change
    its attitude toward him."   45
The hunter went and took with him a courtesan, a prostitute.
They set out on (their) journey (and) went straight forward;
On the third day they reached (their) destination.
The hunter and the courtesan sat down at (this) place.
One day, a second day, they sat opposite the drinking-place.   50
(Then) came the game to the drinking-place to drink.

Tablet I/Column iv

The animals came to the water, (and) their hearts were glad.
And as for him, (for) Enkidu, whose birthplace is the open
     country,
(Who) eats grass with the gazelles,
Drinks with the game at the drinking-place,
(Whose) heart delights with the animals at the water,   5
Him, the wild(?) man, the prostitute saw,
The savage man from the depths of the steppe.
"This is he, wench, naked at your bosom;
Open your lap to him, so that he may succumb to your beauty.
Do not hesitate to approach him;   10
When he sees you, he will approach you.
Undo your robe and let him lie on you.
Stir up lust in him, the woman's task.
All living things, that are nurtured in their habitat, will change
     their feelings towards him,
When he shares his love with you."   15
The courtesan bares her bosom, opens her lap, and he succumbs
     to her beauty.
She does not hesitate to approach him;
She undoes her robe and he lies on her;
She stirs up lust in him, the woman's task,
And he shares his love with her.   20
For six days and seven nights Enkidu mated with the courtesan.
After he was sated with her charms,
He set his face toward his game.
(But) when the gazelles saw him, Enkidu, they ran away;
The game of the steppe fled from his presence.   25
It caused Enkidu to hesitate, rigid was his body.
His knees failed, because his game ran away.
Enki[du] slackened in his running, no longer (could he run)
     as before.
But he had inte[lligence, w]ide was his understanding.
He returned (and) sat at the feet of the courtesan,   30
Looking at the courtesan,
And his ears listening as the courtesan speaks,

[The courtesan] saying to him, to Enkidu:
"[Wi]se art thou, O Enkidu, like a god art thou;
Why dost thou run around with the animals on the steppe?   3
Come, I will lead thee [to] Uruk, the enclosure,
To the holy temple, the dwe[lling] of Anu and Ishtar,
The place where Gilgamesh is, the one perfect in strength,
Who prevails over men like a wild ox."
As she speaks to him, her words find favor;   4
(For) he seeks a friend, one who understands his heart.
Enkidu says to her, the courtesan:
"Come, O prostitute, take me
To the holy temple, the sacred dwelling of Anu (and) Ishtar,
The place where Gilgamesh is, the one perfect in strength,   4
Who prevails over men like a wild ox.
I, I will summon him and [will] speak bold[ly];

Tablet I/Column v

[I will c]ry out in Uruk: 'I am the strong(est)!
[I, yea, I] will change the order of things!
[He who] was born on the steppe is the [strong(est)];
          strength he has!' "
["Come, let us go, that he may see] thy face.
[I will show thee Gilgamesh, where] he is I know well.   5
[Go to Uruk], the enclosure, O Enkidu,
Whe[re peo]ple [array themselves in gorgeous] festal attire,
(Where) [each] day is a holiday.

(Lines 9-12 are badly damaged.)

To thee, O Enkidu, [who rejoi]cest in life,
I will show Gilgamesh, a joyful man.
Look at him, behold his face;   1
Comely is (his) manhood, endowed with vigor is he;
The whole of his body is adorned with [ple]asure.
He has greater strength than thou.
Never does he rest by day or by night.
Enkidu, temper thine arrogance.   2
Gilgamesh—Shamash has conferred favor upon him,

And Anu, Enlil,[10] and Ea[11] have given him a wide under-
    standing.
Before thou wilt arrive from the open country,
Gilgamesh will behold thee in dreams in Uruk."
Indeed, Gilgamesh arose to reveal dreams, saying to his
    mother: 25
"My mother, last night I saw a dream.
There were stars in the heavens;
As if it were the host of heaven[12] (one) fell down to me.
I tried to lift it, but it was too heavy for me;
I tried to move it away, but I could not remove (it).   30
The land of Uruk was standing around [it],
[The land was gathered around it];
[The peop]le [pressed] to[ward it],
[The men th]ronged around it,
[. . .] while my [fell]ows kissed its feet;   35
I bent over it [as] (over) a woman
[And] put it at [thy] feet,
[And thou thyself didst put] it on a par with me."
[The wise, who] is versed in all knowledge, says to her lord;
[Ninsun,[13] the wise], who is versed in all knowledge, says to
    Gilgamesh: 40
"Thi[ne equal(?)] is the star of heaven
Which fell down to thee [as if it were the host of heav]en,
[Which thou didst try to lift but which] was too [hea]vy
    for thee,
[Which thou didst seek to move away but] couldst [not]
    remove,
Which [thou didst put] at my feet,   45
Which [I myself did put on a] par with thee,
(And) over which thou didst be[nd as (over) a woman].

10. God of thunder.
11. God of the earth and water.
12. The stars. The same expression is found in the Bible, e.g., in Isaiah
34:4: "And all the host of heaven shall be dissolved, and the heavens shall
be rolled together as a scroll: and all their host shall fall down . . ."
13. The mother of Gilgamesh.

Tablet I/Column vi

[He is a strong com]panion, one who helps a [friend] in need;
[He is the strong(est) on the steppe]; strength he [has];
(And) [his str]ength is as strong [as (that of) the host of
     heaven].
[That] thou didst be[nd] over him [as (over) a woman],
[Means that he will ne]ver forsake thee.
[This is the meani]ng of thy dream."
[Again Gilgamesh said] to his mother:
"[My mother, I] saw another dream.
[In Uruk, the enclosu]re, there lay an ax, and they were
     gathered about it;
[The la]nd [of Uruk] was standing about it,
[The land was gathe]red around it.
[The peop]le [pressed]toward it,
While I put it at thy feet,
[And] bent over it as (over) a woman,
[And thou thyself] didst put it on a par with me."
The wise, who is versed in all knowledge, says to her son;
[Ninsun, the w]ise, who is versed in all knowledge, says to
     Gilgamesh:
"[The ax] which thou didst see is a man.
That thou didst bend over him as (over) a woman,
[That I myself] did put him on a par with thee,
[Means that he] is a strong companion, one who helps a friend
     in need;
He is [the strong(est) on the steppe]; strength he has;
(And) his strength is as strong [as (that of) the host of
     heav]en."
[Gilgamesh opened his mouth] and said to his mother:
"[. . .] may (this) great [lot] fall to me;
[. . .] that I may have [a companion(?)].
[. . .] I."
[While Gilgamesh revealed] his dreams,
[The courtesan] spoke to Enkidu,
[. . .] the two,
[Enkidu sitting] before her.

[Tablet I of "He who saw everything within the confi]nes(?)
    of the land."
(Colophon:) [. . .] who trusts [in] Ninlil[14]
[. . .] Ashur.

Tablet II

The second tablet of the Assyrian version, which we have followed
so far, is too fragmentary for connected translation, with the exception of a few passages. The text here given is that of the Old
Babylonian version as recorded on the Pennsylvania Tablet. The
first part of this tablet corresponds to column v, lines 25 ff., of Tablet I of the Assyrian version and thus repeats, with certain varia-
tions, some of the lines already given here.

Tablet II/Column i

Gilgamesh arose to reveal the dream,
Saying to his mother:
"My mother, last night
I felt happy and walked about
Among the heroes.   5
There appeared stars in the heavens.
[The h]ost of heaven fell down toward me.
I tried to lift it, but it was too heavy for me;
I tried to move it, but I could not move it.
The land of Uruk was gathered around it,   10
While the heroes kissed its feet.
I put my forehead (firmly) against (it),
And they assisted me.
I lifted it up and carried it to thee."
The mother of Gilgamesh, who is versed in everything,   15
Says to Gilgamesh:
"Truly, O Gilgamesh, one like thee
Has been born on the steppe,
Whom the open country[15] has reared.

14. A goddess, the wife of Enlil.
15. *Shadu*, the word translated as "open country," generally denotes a
mountain or mountainous region. But here it clearly refers to the elevated
region west of Babylonia which, compared to the lowlands of the Tigris-
Euphrates Valley, was indeed quite high.

When thou seest him, thou wilt rejoice [as (over) a woman].   20
The heroes will kiss his feet;
Thou wilt embrace him. . . .
(And) wilt lead him to me."
He lay down and saw another [dream]
(And) said to his mother: 25
"My [mother], I saw another [dream].
[. . .] in the street
[Of Uru]k, the market place,
There lay an ax,
And they were gathered around it.   30
As for the ax itself, its form was different (from that of others).
I looked at it and I rejoiced,
Loving it and bending over it
As (over) a woman.
I took it and put it   35
At my side."
The mother of Gilgamesh, who is versed in everything,
[Says to Gilgamesh]:

(A small break)

Tablet II/Column ii

"Because I shall put him on a par with thee."
While Gilgamesh reveals the dreams,
Enki[du is si]tting before the courtesan.
[. . .] the two.
[Enkidu] forgot where he was born.   5
For six days and seven nights
Enkidu
Mated with the courtesan.
(Then) the co[urtesan] opened her [mouth]
And sa[id] to Enkidu: 10
"I look at thee, O Enkidu, (and) thou art like a god;
Why with the animals
Dost thou range at large over the steppe?
Come, I will lead thee
To [Uruk], the market place,   15

To the holy temple, the dwelling of Anu.
O Enkidu, arise, that I may lead thee
To Eanna, the dwelling of Anu,
Where [Gilgamesh] is, [mighty (?)] in deeds,
And [. . .].   20
Thou [wilt love him like] thyself.
Come, arise from the ground,
[The bed (?)] of the shepherd!"
He listened to her words (and) accepted her advice;
The counsel of the woman   25
He took to heart.[16]
She tore (her) garment in two;
With one she clothed him,
With the other garm[ent]
She clothed herself.   30
She takes his hand
(And) leads him like a [mother]
To the table of the shepherds,
The place of the sheepfold.
The shepherds gathered around him.   35

(About four lines missing)

Tablet II/Column iii

The milk of the wild animals
He was accustomed to suck.
Bread they placed before him;
He felt embarrassed, looked
And stared.   5
Nothing does Enkidu know
Of eating bread,
(And) to drink strong drink
He has not been taught.
The courtesan opened her mouth,   10
Saying to Enkidu:
"Eat the bread, O Enkidu,
(It is) the staff of life;

16. Literally, "Fell upon his heart."

Drink the strong drink, (it is) the fixed custom of the land."
Enkidu ate bread   15
Until he was sated;
(Of) the strong drink he drank
Seven goblets.
His soul felt free (and) happy,
His heart rejoiced,   20
And his face shone.
He rubbed [. . .]
His hairy body;
He anointed himself with oil,
And he became like a human being.   25
He put on a garment,
(And now) he is like a man.
He took his weapon
To attack the lions,
(So that) the shepherds could rest at night.   30
He caught the wolves
(And) captured the lions,
(So that) the great cattle bree[ders] could lie down;
Enkidu was their watchman.
A strong man,   35
A unique hero,
To . . . he said.

(About five lines missing)

Tablet II/Column iv

(About eight lines missing)

He made merry.
He lifted up his eyes   10
And saw a man.
He says to the courtesan:
"Courtesan, bring the man.
Why has he come here?

I wish to know(?) his name."   15
The courtesan called the man
That he might come to him and that he might see him.
"Sir, whither dost thou hasten?
What is (the purpose of) thy painful journey?"
The man opened his mouth   20
And said to En[kidu]:
"To the family house[17] [. . .].
It is the lot of the people.

(Meaning of lines 24-6 is uncertain.)

To the king of Uruk, the market place,
Is open the . . . of the people for the selection of the bride;
To Gilgamesh, the king of Uruk, the market place,
Is open the . . . of the people   30
For the selection of the bride.
He mates with the wives appointed for him.
He comes first.
The husband later.[18]
By the decree of the gods it was pronounced;   35
Since (the day) his umbilical cord was cut
It has been his portion."
At the words of the man
His face grew pale.

(About three lines missing)

Tablet II/Column v

(About six lines missing)

[Enkidu] walks [in front]
And the courtesan [be]hind him.
When he entered Uruk, the market place,
The populace gathered around him.   10
As he stood there in the street

17. The community house, where the men of the town sat.
18. This refers to the "law of the first night."

Of Uruk, the market place,
The people were gathered,
Saying about him:
"He looks like Gilgamesh. . . .   15
He is short(er) in stature,
(But) strong(er) in bo[ne].

. . . .

[He is the strong(est) on the steppe; stren]gth he has.
The milk of the wild animals   20
He used to suck."
Ever in Uruk. . . .
The men rejoiced:
"A mighty one has arisen (as a match)
For the hero whose appearance is (so) handsome;   25
For Gilgamesh an equal
Like a god has arisen."
For Ishhara[19] the bed
Is made.
Gilgamesh [. . .],   30
At night [. . .].
As he approaches,
[Enkidu] sta[nds] in the street
To blo[ck the pa]ssage
To Gilgamesh   35
[. . .] with his strength.

(About three lines missing)

Tablet II/Column vi

(About five lines missing)

Gilgamesh [. . .]
On the steppe(?) [. . .]
Sprouts [. . .].
He arose and [went]
To him.   10
They met on the market place of the land;

19. A goddess of love, probably a form of Ishtar.

Enkidu blocked the gate
With his foot,
Not permitting Gilgamesh to enter.
They grappled with each other,   15
Snorting(?) like bull(s);
They shattered the doorpost,
That the wall shook.
(Yea), Gilgamesh and Enkidu
Grappled with each other,   20
Snorting(?) like bull(s);
They shattered the doorpost,
That the wall shook.

A fragment of the Assyrian recension has:

At the door of the family house Enkidu blocked (the entrance)
    with [his] feet,
Not permitting (them) to bring in Gilgamesh.
They grappled with each other in the doorway of the family
    house.
They fought together on the street, the market place(?) of the
    land;
They [shatt]ered(?) [the doorpost], that the wall shook.   50

The Old Babylonian version continues:

Gilgamesh bent over,
With his foot on the ground,[20]
His fury abated,
And he turned away.[21]
After he has turned away,
Enkidu says to him,
To Gilgamesh: 30
"As one unique (among men) thy mother,
The wild cow[22] of the enclosures,

20. This means that Gilgamesh won the wrestling match. Gilgamesh real-
izes that Enkidu could be a valuable companion to him and therefore
forms a friendship with him.
21. Literally "he turned his breast."
22. A poetical term for "the strong one."

Ninsunna,
Did bear thee.
Thy head is exalted above (all other) men;   35
The kingship over the people
Enlil has decreed for thee."
The second tablet.

(Catch-line:) [Thy . . .] surpasses.

Tablet III

Of this tablet we again have two recensions, an Old Babylonian
and an Assyrian. The Old Babylonian recension is inscribed on the
Yale Tablet. It continues the story of the Pennsylvania Tablet,
which we have just considered, and belongs to the same edition of
the epic.

A.   THE OLD BABYLONIAN VERSION

Tablet III / Column i

The beginning of the column is destroyed. When the text becomes
legible, Gilgamesh has already decided upon an expedition against
Huwawa (Humbaba), who dwells in the cedar forest. Enkidu tries
to dissuade him.

"[Why] dost thou desire
[To do this thing]?
[. . .] very   15
[. . .] [thou de]sirest
[To go down(?)] [to the fo]rest.
A message [. . .]."
They kissed one another
And formed a friendship   20

(Break)

Tablet III / Column ii

(Lines 58-60 almost completely destroyed.)

The mother of [Gilgamesh, who is versed in everything],
[Raised her hands] befo[re Shamash].

(Break)

The eyes [of Enkidu filled] with tea[rs];
He [felt ill] at heart
[And] sighed [bitterly].
[Yea, the eyes of En]kidu filled with tears; 75
[He felt ill] at heart
And sighed [bitterly].
[Gilgamesh tur]ned his face (toward him)
[And said] to Enkidu:
"[My friend, why] do thine eyes 80
[Fill with tea]rs?
(Why) dost thou [feel (so) ill at heart]
[And] sig[h (so) bitterly]?"
En[kidu opened his mouth]
And said to Gilgamesh: 85
"My friend, . . .
Have bound(?) my sinews(?).
Mine arms have lost their power;
My strength has become weak."
Gilgamesh opened his mouth 90
And said to Enkidu:

Tablet III/Column iii

(Break)

"[In the forest dwells] terrible [Hu]wawa.
[Let us, me and thee, ki]ll [him],
[And let us des]troy [all the evil in the land]."

(Lines 99-102 are too fragmentary for translation.)

Enkidu opened his mouth
And said to Gilgamesh:
"I learned (it), my friend, 105
When I was (still) ranging at large over the open country with
the game.
To (a distance of) ten thousand double-hours the forest
extends(?) in each (direction).

[Who is it that] would go down into its interior?
[Huwa]wa—his roaring is (like that of) a flood-storm,
His mouth is fire,   110
His breath is death!
(So) why dost thou desire
To do this thing?
An irresistible onslaught is
The . . . of Huwawa."   115
Gilgamesh opened his mouth
And [sai]d to Enkidu:
"The mountain [of the ce]dar I will climb!"

(Lines 119-26 are almost completely destroyed.)

Enkidu opened his mouth
And said t[o Gilgamesh]:
"How shall we go
To the [cedar] forest?   130
Its guardian, Gilgamesh, is a war[rior];
He is strong (and) never does he s[leep]."

(Lines 133-5 are badly mutilated.)

Tablet III/Column iv

To preserve [the cedar forest],
[Enlil has appointed him] as a sevenfold(?) terror."

A fragment belonging to the fifth column of the second tablet of
the Assyrian version contains the following lines:

"To preserve the cedar [fore]st,
Enlil has appointed him as a terror to mortals.
Humbaba—his roaring is (like that of) a flood-storm, his mouth
    is fire, his breath is death!
At sixty double-hours he can hear the wild cows of his forest;
    who is it that would go down to his forest?
To preserve the cedar, Enlil has appointed him as a terror to
    mortals.   5
And on him who goes down to his forest weakness takes hold."

The Old Babylonian recension continues:

Gilgamesh opened his mouth
[And] said to [Enkidu]:
"Who, my friend, . . . ?   140
Only the gods d[well] forever with Shamash.
(But) as for mankind, their days are numbered.
Whatever they do is but wind!
Already here[23] thou art afraid of death.
What has become of thy heroic power?   145
I will go before thee.
Thy mouth may (then) call to me: 'Approach! Be not afraid!'
If I fall, I will establish a name for myself!
'Gilgamesh is fallen!' (they will say). '(In combat)
With terrible Huwawa!'   150

(Lines 151-6 are badly mutilated.)

[Thus call]ing to me thou hast afflicted my heart.
(But) [I will] put [my hand] (to it)
And [will cu]t down the cedar.
An everlasting [name] I will establish for myself! 160
[Orders(?)], my friend, to the armorer I will give(?);
[Weapons] they shall cast in our presence."
[Orders(?)] to the armorers they gave (?).
The craftsmen sat down (and) held a conference.
Great weapons they cast.   165
Axes of three talents[24] each they cast.
Great swords they cast,
With blades of two talents each,
With the pommels(?) on the hilt(?) (weighing) thirty pounds
    each,
With golden sword [sheaths(?)] (weighing) thirty pounds
    each.   170
Gilgamesh and Enkidu were equipped with ten talents each.
In [Uru]k's [ga]te, with its seven bolts,
[. . .] . . . the populace gathered.
[. . .] . . . in the street of Uruk, the market place.

23. I.e., while we are still in Uruk.
24. One talent equals sixty pounds.

[. . .] . . . Gilgamesh.   175
[The elders of Uruk], the market place,
[. . . sa]t down before him,
[While Gilgamesh s]poke [thus]:
"[Hearken, O elders of Uruk, the m]arket place!
[.   .   .   .   ]   180

Tablet III/Column v

Him of whom they talk I, Gilgamesh, want to see.
Him with whose name the lands are filled,
Him I will vanquish in the cedar forest.
How strong the offspring of Uruk is,
That I will cause the land to hear!   185
I will put my hand (to it) and will cut down the cedar.
An everlasting name I will establish for myself!"
The elders of Uruk, the market place,
Replied to Gilgamesh:
"Thou art young, O Gilgamesh, and thy heart has carried thee
      away.   190
Thou dost not know what thou proposest to do.
We hear Huwawa's appearance is different (from that of
      others).[25]
Who is there th[at can wit]hstand his weapons?
To (a distance of) ten thous[and double-hours] the forest
      extends(?) in each (direction).
Who is it w[ho would go] down into its interior?   195
As for Huwawa, his roar is (like that of) a flood-storm.
His mouth is fire and his breath is death.
Why dost thou desire to do this thing?
An irresistible onslaught is the . . . of Huwawa."
When Gilgamesh heard the words of his counselors,   200
He looked at [his] friend and laughed.

The next few lines contained a speech of Gilgamesh directed to his
friend Enkidu. Unfortunately, almost every word of it has been
lost. When the text again becomes connected, the elders of the city
are addressing Gilgamesh.

25. Different, and therefore terrifying.

"May thy (tutelary) god [protect] thee.
On the road (home) may he cause [thee to return in sa]fety.
To the quay of Uru[k may he cause thee to return]."
Gilgamesh prostrated himself [before Shamash]: 215
"The words which they speak [. . .].
I go, O Shamash; [to thee I raise my] hands.
May it then be well with [my] soul.
Bring me back to the quay of [Uruk].
Place [over me] (thy) protection." 220
Gilgamesh called [his friend]
[And consulted] his omen.

The omen appears to have been unfavorable; for, after a break, the text continues:

Tablet III/Column vi

Tears are running down [the face] of Gilgamesh.
"[. . .] a road which I have never [traveled]." 230

(Lines 231-5 are almost completely destroyed.)

[They brought(?)] his weapons.
[. . .] mighty [swor]ds,
[Bow] and quiver
They placed [into] (his) hands.
[He] took the axes, 240
[. . .] his quiver,
[The bow] of Anshan.[26]
[He put his sw]ord in his girdle.
[. . .] they marched.
[The people(?)] approach(?) Gilgamesh, 245
[Saying: "When] wilt thou return to the city?"
[The eld]ers bless him;
[For] the journey they counsel Gilgamesh:
"[Do not t]rust in thy strength, O Gilgamesh!
Let him lead the way and spare thyself; 250
[Let] Enkidu go before thee.

26. A district in southern Elam, east of Babylonia, in present-day southwest Iran.

He has seen the [wa]y, has trodden the road
[To(?)] the entrance of the forest.
[. . .] Huwawa. . . .
[He who goes b]efore will save the companion;   255
Let him lead the [way and spare thyself].
[May] Shamash [cause] thee [to gain] thy victory.
May he make thine eyes see what thy mouth has spoken.
May he open for thee the closed path.
May he open a road for thy treading;   260
May he open the mountain for thy foot.
May the night bring thee things over which thou wilt rejoice.
May Lugalbanda[27] stand by thee
In thy victory.
Gain thy victory as (over) a child.   265
In the river of Huwawa, toward whom thou strivest,
Wash thy feet.
At eventide dig a well;
Let there always be pure water in thy waterskin;
Offer [co]ld water to Shamash.   270
Be thou [ever] mindful of Lugalbanda."
[Enkid]u opened his mouth and said to Gilgamesh:
"[. . .] . . . set out on (thy) journey.
[Let not] thy heart be afraid; look at me.
. . . .
[The road whi]ch Huwawa is wont to travel.   275
[. . .] command them to return (home)."

The next seven lines, in which Gilgamesh addressed the elders, are
too fragmentary for translation.

[When they heard] this speech of his,   285
They [set] the hero on (his) way:
"Go, Gilgamesh, [. . .];
May thy (tutelary) god walk [at thy side].
May he let [thine eyes] see [what thy mouth has spoken]."

The Old Babylonian version breaks off after three more badly

27. The consort of Gilgamesh's mother, Ninsun, and the tutelary god of
Gilgamesh.

mutilated lines. The story is continued, however, in the Assyrian version, which sets in after line 247, repeating some of the material which we have already gone over.

B. THE ASSYRIAN VERSION

Tablet III/Column i

[The elders opened their mouths and said to Gilgamesh]:
"Gilgamesh, do not trust in the abundance of [thy] strength.
Let thy . . . be satisfied. . . .
He who goes before safeguards the companion;
He who knows the way protects his friend.   5
Let Enkidu go before thee.
He knows the way to the cedar forest.
He has seen conflict and is experienced in warfare.
Let Enkidu protect the friend, safeguard the companion.
Let him bring his body over the ditches.[28]   10
In our assembly we have paid heed to thee, O king;
In return, pay thou heed to us, O king!"
Gilgamesh opened his mouth and spoke,
Saying to Enkidu:
"Come, my friend, let us go to (the temple) Egalmah   15
Before Ninsun, the great queen!
Ninsun, the wise, who is versed in all knowledge,
Will recommend (well-)counseled steps for our feet."
They took each other by the hand,
Gilgamesh and Enkidu, as they went to Egalmah   20
Before Ninsun, the great queen.
Gilgamesh set about and entered [. . .]:
"Ninsun, I will tell [thee . . .],
A far journey, to the pla[ce of Humbaba].
A b[attl]e which I do not kno[w I am about to face].   25
[A road] which [I do] not [know I am about to travel].
[Until] the da[y that I go and return],
[Until I reach the cedar forest],
[Until I slay fierce Humbaba]

28. Perhaps around the cedar forest.

[And destroy from the land all the evil which Shamash abhors],   30
[Pray thou to Shamash for me]!"

(The remainder of the break cannot be restored)

Tablet III/Column ii

[Ninsun e]ntered [her chamber].
[. . .]   . . . .
[She put on a garment] as befitted her body;
[She put on an ornament] as befitted her breast;
[She put on a . . .] and was covered with her tiara.   5
[. . .] ground. . . .
. . . [. . .] she went up on the roof.
She went up to [. . .] Shamash (and) offered incense.
She brought the offe[ring and] raised her hands before
    Shamash:
"Why didst thou give [my] son Gilgamesh (such) a restless
    heart (and) endow him (with it)?   10
And now thou hast touched him, and he goes
On a far journey, to the place of Humbaba,
To face a battle which he does not know,
To travel a road which he does not know.
Until the day that he goes and returns,   15
Until he reaches the cedar forest,
Until he kills fierce Humbaba
And destroys from the land all the evil which thou abhorrest,
The day that thou . . .
. . . may Aya, (thy) bride, remind thee (of it).   20
In[trust(?)] him to the watchmen of the night.

Here occurs a big gap. Virtually every word up to column iv, line
15, is destroyed.

Tablet III/Column iv

She[29] extinguished(?) the incense and . [. . .].   15
Enkidu she called and [gave (him) information]:
"Strong Enkidu, (who) art not the offspring of my lap,

29. Ninsun, the mother of Gilgamesh.

I have now adopted(?) thee,
With the gifts(?) of Gilgamesh,
The priestesses, the hierodules, [and the vo]taries."   20
. . . she placed around Enkidu's neck.

The rest of the column is too fragmentary for translation. The next
column is almost completely destroyed. Also the beginning of column vi is gone. In the remaining lines of the tablet the elders of
the city again address Gilgamesh.

Tablet III/Column vi

"Let [Enkidu] pr[otect the friend, safeguard the companion].
[Let him bring his body] over the ditches.
In our assembly [we have paid heed to thee, O king];   10
In return, p[ay thou heed to us, O king]!"
Enkidu opened his mouth [and spoke],
Saying [to Gilgamesh]:
"My friend, tu[rn . . .]
A way not [. . .]."   15

(Remainder of the tablet broken away)

Tablet IV

The first four columns of the Assyrian version are lost. They un-
doubtedly contained a record of the journey to the cedar forest.
Part of such a record is found on the following fragment from
Uruk, inscribed in Babylonian.

Tablet IV/Column i

[After twenty] double-hours[30] they ate[31] a morsel;
[After thi]rty (additional) double-hours they stopped for the
    night.
[Fifty double-hou]rs they walked all day.
[The stretch of a mo]nth and fifteen days [they covered(?)] in
    three days.

30. Or *beru*, a measure of distance as well as time. One *beru* represented
the distance a man could walk in two hours' time.
31. Literally, "broke off."

[Before Shamash] they dug [a well].[32]   5

(Break)

Tablet IV/Column ii

After twenty double-hours they a[te a morsel];
After thirty (additional) double-hours they [stopped for the
    night].
Fifty double-hours they wa[lked all day].
The stretch of a month [and fifteen days they covered(?) in
    three days].

(Break)

Another fragment from Uruk repeats the same words, with the
addition of the following lines, which in part have been restored
from Tablet V.

Gilgamesh [ascended the mountain],
[He] poured out [his fine-meal . . .]:   15
"[Mountain, bring] a dream with [favorable] meaning."

Tablet IV/Column v

When the Assyrian version again sets in, Gilgamesh and Enkidu
have arrived at the gate of the forest, which is guarded by a watchman placed there by Humbaba. At the sight of the watchman Gilgamesh apparently loses his courage, for Enkidu calls out to him:

"[Remember what] thou didst say [in] Uruk!
[Arise] and stand forth [that thou mayest kill him].   40
[. . . Gil]gamesh, the offspring of Ur[uk . . .]."
[Gilgamesh he]ard the word of [his] mouth and was full of
    confidence.
"[Hur]ry (now), step up to him [. . .].
[. . . g]o down into the forest and [. . .].
[He is] wont to put on seven coats of mail(?) [. . .][33]   45
[One he has just] put on, six of them are (still) doffed [. . .]."

32. Compare Tablet III, lines 268-70 (Old Babylonian version).
33. Apparently magical shirts which make the watchman invulnerable.

Like a furious wild ox [. . .].
. . . he withdrew and was full of [. . .].
The watchman of the woods calls out [. . .].
Humbaba like . . . [. . .].   50

Tablet IV/Column vi

The beginning of this column is wanting. The missing portion evidently related the story of the combat between the two heroes and the watchman and Enkidu's unfortunate act of opening the enchanted gate with his bare hands.

[Enkidu] opened his [mouth] and sp[oke, saying to
     Gilgamesh]:
"[My friend, let us not] go down [into the forest].
[When] I opened [the gate, my hand] became paralyzed(?)."   25
[Gilgam]esh opened his mouth and spoke, saying [to Enkidu]:
"[. . .] my friend, like a weakling [. . .].
[. . . we] have traversed, all(?) of them [. . .].
. . . .
[My friend], (who art) experienced in warfare, [skilful]
     in battle,   30
[. . .] touch and thou wilt not be afraid of [death(?)].
[. . .] and remain(?) with me [. . .].
[. . .] . . . . ,
So that the paralysis(?) of thy hand may depart and the weakness pass [. . .].
[Would] my friend want to remain(?) here? Let us go [down]
     (into the depths of the forest) together;   35
[Let] the combat [not diminish(?)] thy courage; forget death
     and [. . .].
[. . .] a man ready for action(?) and circumspect.
[He who] goes [before] protects his person, may he (also)
     safeguard the companion.
[When] they fall, they have established a name for themselves."
[At the gr]een [mountain] they arrived together;   40
[Stilled into si]lence were their words, (and) they themselves
     stood still.
(Catch-line:)   They [stood still] and looked(?) at the forest.

Tablet V/Column i

They stood still and looked(?) at the forest.
They beheld the height of the cedar.
They beheld the entrance to the forest.
Where Humbaba was wont to walk there was a path;
Straight were the tracks and good was the passage.   5
They beheld the mountain of the cedar, the dwelling-place of
    the gods, the throne-dais of Irnini.[34]
The cedar uplifted its fulness before the mountain;
Fair was its shade (and) full of delight;
[Cov]ered was the brushwood (and) covered the [. . .].

After a few more badly mutilated lines the description of the won-
ders of the cedar forest unfortunately breaks off. The next column
is destroyed almost in its entirety. The sense does not become connected until about the middle of the third column.

Tablet V/Column iii

"[The second dr]eam which I sa[w . . .].[35]
[Within] (deep) mountain gorges [we were standing(?)].
[A mountain] fell [. . .].
[In comparison to it(?), we were] like a little 'fly of the
    canebrakes.' "   35
[He who] was born on the step[pe . . .],
Enkidu, [said] to his friend, as he [interpreted the dream]:
"My [frie]nd, [thy] dream is favorable [. . .];
[The dr]eam is excellent [. . .].
My [frie]nd, the mountain which thou didst see [is Humbaba].   40
[We] shall seize Humbaba, we [shall kill him],
And [shall throw] his body on the plain.
. . . morning . . . [. . .]."

A similar dream, if not simply a different version of the same
dream, is recorded on the obverse of the Semitic recension from
Boghazkoy. The beginning of the tablet is destroyed. When the text
becomes intelligible we read:

34. A goddess, probably a form of Ishtar.
35. Gilgamesh is speaking.

They took each other's (hand and) went to retire for the night. 5
Sleep, the outpouring of the night, overcame [them].
At midnight the sleep [departed] from him.[36]
The dream he told to Enkidu, [his fri]end.
"If thou didst not wake me, what [has wakened me]?
Enkidu, my friend, I have seen a [second] dream.   10
If thou didst wake me, what [. . .]?
In addition to my first dream [I have seen] a second.
In my dream, my friend, a mountain [toppled];
It struck me, caught my feet [. . .].
The light became glaringly strong, a unique ma[n appeared]. 15
His grace was (the most) beautiful in (all) the land.
He pulled me out from under the mountain.
He gave me water to drink, and my heart fel[t at ease].
On the ground he set [my] feet [. . .]."
Enkidu said to this god,[37] [speaking]   20
To Gilgamesh: "My friend, let us g[o down into the plain to
    take counsel together(?)]."

The interpretation of the dream is lost, for after a few more fragmentary lines the obverse breaks off. The Assyrian version goes on:

[After] twenty double-hours they broke [off a morsel];
After thirty (additional) double-hours they stopped [for the
    night];   45
Before Shamash they dug a well [. . .].
Gilgamesh ascended [the mountain].
He poured out his fine-meal [. . .].
"Mountain, bring a dream [for Enkidu].
Make for him [. . .]!"   50

Tablet V / Column iv

[The mountain] brought a dr[eam for Enkidu].
[He m]ade for him [. . .].
A cold shower [passe]d by, [. . .] . . .
[It caused] him to cower and [. . .]

36. From Gilgamesh.
37. To Gilgamesh, who in this passage is expressly called a god.

[. . .] and like the grain of the mountains [. . .].   5
[Gi]lgamesh supports his chin on [his] knees.
[Sle]ep, such as is shed upon mankind, fell on him.
[In] the middle (of the night) he ended his sleep.
He arose and said to his friend:
"My friend, didst thou not call me? Why did I wake up?   10
Didst thou not touch me? Why am I frightened?
Did no god pass by? Why are my members benumbed (with
    fear)?
My friend, I saw a third dream;
And the dream which I saw was altogether frightful.
The heavens roared, the earth resounded;   15
Daylight failed, darkness came;
Lightning [flash]ed, fire blazed;
[The clouds] thickened(?), raining death.
The brightness [vani]shed, the fire went out;
[And that which] fell down, turned to ashes.   20
[Let us go] down into the plain that we may take counsel
    together."
Enkidu [heard] his dream and interpreted it, saying to
    Gilgamesh:

The remainder of the Assyrian column is lost. The missing portion
probably related that Enkidu put a favorable interpretation on the
dream of his friend, whereupon both of them resolved to cut down
the cedar, for the Hittite recension has:

[Gilgamesh] took [the ax in his hand]
[And] cut down [the cedar].
[But when Huwawa] heard the noise(?),
He became enraged (and said):   "Who has come   10
[And disturbed the trees that] have grown up on my mountains,
And has cut down the cedar?"
[Then] the heavenly Shamash spoke to them
From heaven: "Approach,
Be not afraid [. . .]!"   15

After a few more fragmentary lines of uncertain meaning the tablet unfortunately breaks off. What happened we do not know; but

apparently something did not turn out according to expectations, for another Hittite fragment continues:

His tears [gushed forth] in streams.
And Gilgamesh [said] to the heavenly Shamash:

(Lines 8-9 are badly damaged.)

"I have [followed] the he[aven]ly Shamash,   10
And have pursued the road de[creed for me]."
The heavenly Shamash heard the prayer of Gilgamesh;
And mighty winds arose against Huwawa:
The great wind, the north wind, [the south wind, the whirl-
     wind],
The storm wind, the chill wind, the tempe[stuous] wind,   15
The hot wind; eight winds arose against him
And beat against the eyes of [Huwawa].
He is unable to go forward,
He is unable to turn back.
So Huwawa gave up.   20
Then Huwawa said to Gilgamesh:
"Let me go, Gilgamesh; thou [shalt be] my [master],
And I will be thy servant. And [the trees]
That I have grown (on my mountains),
. . . [. . .],   25
[I will] cut down and [build thee] houses."
But Enkidu [said] to [Gilgamesh]:
"Do not [hearken] to the w[ord] which Huwawa [has spoken];
Huwawa [must] not [remain alive]!"

Here the Hittite text again breaks off. Of the Assyrian version a few more lines, belonging to columns v and vi, have been preserved, but they are too badly damaged for translation. All we can conclude from them is that Gilgamesh and Enkidu cut off the head of Humbaba and that the expedition had a successful issue. The two friends then returned to Uruk.

Tablet VI

He[38] washed his long hair (and) polished his weapons.
The hair of his head he threw back over his shoulders.

38. Gilgamesh.

He threw off his soiled (clothes and) put on his clean ones.

He clothed himself with *asitu*-garments and fastened (them)
with an *aguhhu*.[39]

When Gilgamesh put on his tiara,   5

Great Ishtar lifted (her) eyes to the beauty of Gilgamesh.

"Come, Gilgamesh, be thou my consort.

Grant me thy fruit as a gift.

Be thou my husband and I will be thy wife!

I will cause to be harnessed for thee a chariot of lapis lazuli and
gold,   10

Whose wheels are gold and whose horns are . . .

Storm-demons (for) great mules thou shalt hitch (to it).

Amid the fragrance of cedar thou shalt enter our house.

(And) when thou enterest our house,

Threshold (and) dais shall kiss thy feet.   15

Before thee shall bow down kings, rulers, (and) princes.

[The yield(?)] of mountain and plain they shall bring thee in
tribute.

Thy goats shall bear triplets, thy sheep twins.

Thy burden-carrying donkey shall overtake the mule.

Thy chariot horses shall be famous for (their) running.   20

[Thine ox] in the yoke shall have no rival."

[Gilgamesh] opened his mouth and said,

[Addressing] great Ishtar:

["But what must I give] thee, if I take thee in marriage?

[I must give (thee) oil] and clothing for (thy) body.   25

[I must give thee] bread and victuals.

[. . .] food fit for divinity.

[. . . drin]k fit for royalty.

(Lines 29-31 are almost completely destroyed.)

[What will be my advantage if] I take thee in marriage?

[Thou art but a . . . which does not . . .] in the cold(?);

A back door [which does not] keep out blast or windstorm;

A palace which crus[hes] the heroes (within it);   35

An elephant [that shakes off(?)] his carpet;

39. *Asitu:* fringed; and *aguhhu:* a sash.

Pitch which [dirties] him who carries it;
A waterskin which [wets] him who carries it;
A limestone which [. . .] a stone rampart;
A jasper(?) [. . .] the enemy country;   40
A sandal which [causes] its wearer to t[rip(?)].
What lover [of thine is there whom thou dost love] forever?
What shepherd(?) of thine [is there] who can please [thee for
    all time]?
Come, and I will un[fold(?) thee the tale] of thy lovers.

. . . .   45

For Tammuz, thy [youth]ful husband,
Thou hast decreed wailing year after year.[40]
The variegated roller thou didst love.
(Yet) thou didst smite him and break his wing.
(Now) he stands in the groves, crying 'Kappi!'[41]   50
Thou didst love the lion, perfect in strength.
(But) thou didst dig for him seven and yet seven pits.
Thou didst love the horse, magnificent in battle.
(Yet) thou hast decreed for him the whip, the spur, and the
    thong.
To run seven double-hours thou hast decreed for him.   55
Thou hast decreed for him to trouble (the water before) drink-
    ing (it).
For his mother Silili thou hast decreed lamentation.
Thou didst love the shepherd of the herd,
[Who] without ceasing heaped up charcoals for thee
And [dai]ly sacrificed kids unto thee.   60
(Yet) [thou didst s]mite him and turn him into a wolf.
His own herd boys (now) chase him away,
And his dogs bite his shanks.
Thou didst love Ishullanu, thy father's palm-gardener,
Who without ceasing brought thee date-bunches(?)   65

40. These lines refer to the annual festival of wailing for Tammuz, the god
of vegetation, who was believed to descend to the underworld each autumn
and to return with the advent of spring. This festival was still celebrated
in Biblical times: see Ezekiel 8:14.
41. The roller bird, so called because during the breeding season it per-
forms loops and rolls in flight, utters a hoarse cry resembling the Babylonian expression *kappi*, meaning "my wing."

And daily provided thy table with plenty.
Thou didst cast (thine) eyes on him and didst go to him,
   (saying):
'O Ishullanu of mine, come, let us enjoy thy vigor.
Put forth thy hand and touch our waist.'
Ishullanu said to thee: 70
'What dost thou ask of me?
Does my mother not bake? Have I not eaten,
That I should eat bread (that brings) evil(?) and curses?
(And) against the frost the bulrushes [afford sufficient]
   protection!'
When thou didst hear this [his speech],   75
Thou didst smite him (and) tran[sform him] into a mole(?).
Thou didst cause him to dwell in the middle of . . . [. . .].
He does not ascend the . . . , he does not go down . . . .
And if thou wilt love me, thou wilt [treat me like] unto them."
When Ishtar [heard] this,   80
Ishtar burst into a rage and [ascended] to heaven.
Ishtar went before Anu, [her father];
She we[nt] before Antum, her mother, [and said]:
"My father, Gilgamesh has cursed me.
Gilgamesh has enumerated mine evil deeds(?),   85
Mine evil deeds(?) and my cur[ses]."[42]
Anu opened his mouth and said,
Speaking to great Ishtar:
"Thou thyself didst invite the . . . [. . .];
And so Gilgamesh enumerated thine evil deeds(?),   90
Thine evil deeds(?) and [thy] cur[ses]."
Ishtar opened her mouth and said,
Speaking to [Anu, her father]:
"My father, create for me the bull of heaven [that he may
   destroy Gilgamesh]!
Fill Gil[gamesh with . . .].   95
(But) if [thou wilt not create] for me the bull of [heaven],
I will sm[ash the door of the underworld and break the bolt];
I will let [the door stand wide open(?)];

42. The misfortunes which she has brought on her former lovers.

I will cause [the dead to rise that they may eat as the living],[43]
[So that the dead will be] more [numerous than the living]!"　100
A[nu opened his mouth and said],
Speaking [to gre]at Ish[tar]:
"[If I do what] thou desirest of [me],
[There will be] seven years of (empty) st[raw].
Hast [thou] gathered [(enough) grain for the people]?　105
Hast [thou] grown (enough) fodder [for the cattle]?
[Ishtar opened her mouth] and said,
[Speaking to A]nu, her father:
"I have heaped up [grain for the people],
I have grown [fodder for the cattle].　110
[If there will be seven] years of (empty) straw,
[I have] gathered [(enough) grain for the people],
[And I have grown (enough)] fodder [for the cattle]."

The next eight lines are extremely fragmentary. It is clear, however, that Anu finally acceded to Ishtar's demand, for the epic continues:

[The bull of heaven] descended [. . .].
With his [first] snort [he killed a hundred men].
Two hundred men [. . . three hundred] men.　125
With [his] second snort [he killed a hundred . . .] in
　addition(?),
Two hundred men [. . . in addition(?) . . .] three hundred
　men
[. . .] in addition(?).
With [his] third snort [. . . h]e attacked(?) Enkidu.
(But) Enkidu . . . his onslaught.　130
Enkidu leaped and sei[zed] the bull of heaven by [his] horns.
The bull of heaven foamed at the mouth.
With the thick of his tail[. . .].
Enkidu opened his mouth an[d said],
Speaking [to Gilgamesh]:　135
"My friend, we boasted [. . .]."

43. And so consume the nourishment which would otherwise have been offered the gods.

(Lines 137-44 are too fragmentary for translation.)

And [betw]een the na[pe] (and) his [horn]s [. . .].   14

.   .   .   .

Enkidu chased (him) and [. . .] the bull of heaven.
[He sei]zed him by [the thick of] his [ta]il.

(Lines 149-51 are badly damaged.)

Between the nape (and) the horns [he thrust] his sword
     [. . .].
When they had killed the bull of heaven, they to[re out his]
     heart
(And) placed (it) before Shamash.
They stepped back and prostrated themselves before Shamash.   15
The two brothers sat down.
Ishtar went up on the wall of Uruk, the enclosure;
She ascended to the (rampart's) crest(?) and uttered a curse:
"Woe unto Gilgamesh, who has besmirched me (and) has killed
     the bull of heaven!"
When Enkidu heard this speech of Ishtar,   16
He tore out the right thigh of the bull of heaven and tossed (it)
     before her, (saying):
"If only I could get hold of thee,
I would do unto thee as unto him;
(Or) I would tie his entrails to thy side!"
Ishtar assembled the girl-devotees,   16
The prostitutes, and the courtesans;
Over the right thigh of the bull of heaven she set up a
     lamentation.
But Gilgamesh called the craftsmen, the armorers,
All of them.
The artisans admired the size of the horns.   17
Thirty pounds each was their content of lapis lazuli.
Two inches was their thickness.
Six *gur*[44] of oil, the capacity of the two,
He presented as ointment to his (tutelary) god, Lugalbanda.

44. In the period to which the Gilgamesh epic dates back, one Babylonian
gur was equal to about 65 gallons.

He brought (them) into the room of his rulership(?) and hung
    (them) up (therein).   175
In the Euphrates they washed their hands.
They took each other's (hand) and went away.
They rode through the street of Uruk.
The people of Uruk were gathered to see [them].
Gilgamesh says (these) words   180
To the maids(?) of U[ruk(?)]:
"Who is the (most) glorious among heroes?
Who is the (most) eminent among men?"
"Gilgamesh is the (most) glorious among heroes!
[Gilgamesh is the (most) emine]nt among men!"   185

(Lines 186-8 are too badly damaged for translation.)

Gilgamesh celebrated a joyful feast in his palace.
The heroes lay down, resting on (their) night couches.   190
Also Enkidu lay down, and saw a dream.
Enkidu arose, to reveal the dream,
Saying to his friend:
"My friend, why did the great gods take counsel together?"

(Colophon:)

Tablet VI of "He who saw everything," of the series of
    Gilgamesh.   195
Written down according to its original and collated.

Tablet VII/Column i

With the exception of the first line, preserved as the catch-line on
the preceding tablet (line 194), the beginning of the seventh tablet
of the Assyrian version is lost. Fortunately, however, it can be supplied from the Hittite recension.

[. . .] . . . Then came the day.
[And] Enkidu said to Gilgamesh:
"[My friend, hear] what a drea[m I had] last night.
Anu, Enlil, Ea, and the heavenly Shamash [took counsel to-
    gether].
And Anu said to Enlil: 5

'Because they have killed the bull of heaven and have killed
    Huwa[wa],
[That one of the two shall die],' said Anu,
'Who stripped the mountains of the cedar!'
But Enlil said: 'Enkidu shall die;
Gilgamesh shall not die!'
Now the heavenly Shamash replied to Enlil, the hero:
'Have they not killed the bull of heaven and Huwawa at my
    command?
And now the innocent Enkidu shall die?'
But Enlil was enraged
At the heavenly Shamash (and said):
'Because daily thou descendest to them as though thou wert one
    of their own(?)!'"
E[nkidu] lay (ill) before Gilgamesh.
And as his tears gushed forth in streams,
(Gilgamesh said to him):   "My brother, my dear brother, why
    do they acquit me instead of thee?"
Moreover (he said):   "Shall I sit down by the spirit of the
    dead,
At the door(?) of the spirit of the dead?
And [shall I] never (again) [see] my dear brother with mine
    eyes?"

The remainder of the Hittite text is wanting. As Enkidu is lying
on his sickbed, knowing that the end is near, he evidently reviews
his life and feels that it would have been far better if he had remained on the steppe and had never been introduced to civilization,
for what has it brought him? In his distress he curses the gate that
lamed his hand, he curses the hunter who brought the courtesan to
him, and then he curses the courtesan herself for having lured him
to Uruk. The Assyrian version, after a break, relates these episodes
as follows.

Enki[du . . .] lifted up [his eyes].
With the gate he speaks as if [it were human],
(Although) the gate of the forest is irra[tional]
(And) has no understanding [. . .]:
"At (a distance of) twenty double-hours I admired thy timber
    [. . .].

Till I sighted the towering cedar [. . .].
There was nothing strange about thy timber [. . .].
Seventy-two cubits was thy height, twenty-four cubits thy
    breadth [. . .].
Thy . . . , thy . . . , and thy . . . [. . .].
Thy craftsman(?) made thee in Nippur [. . .].
O gate, had I known that this was [thy purpose],
And that [thy] beauty [would bring on] this (disaster),
I would have lifted an ax (and) [shattered thee all]!
I would have constructed a reed frame [out of thee]!"

Gap of about fifty lines. Enkidu now calls upon Shamash to curse
the hunter.

Tablet VII/Column iii

"[. . .] his possession(s) destroy, his power decrease.
[May] his [wa]y [be unacceptable] before thee.
May [the game which he tries to trap] escape from him.
[. . . may] the hunter [not obt]ain the desire of his heart."
[His heart] prompted him to curse (also) [the courte]san, the
    prostitute.   5
"[Co]me, O prostitute, thy de[stin]y I will decree,
[A des]tiny that shall not end for all eternity.
[I will] curse thee with a mighty curse.
[. . .] may its curses rise up early against thee.

(Lines 10-18 are too fragmentary for translation.)

[. . .] the street shall be thy dwelling-place.
[The shade of the wall shall be] thine abode.   20
[. . .] thy feet.
[May the drunken and the thirsty (alike) smite] thy cheek."

(Lines 23-32 are too fragmentary for translation.)

When Shamash heard [the word]s of his mouth,
He forthwith called him [from] heaven:
"Why, O Enkidu, dost thou curse the courtesan, the prostitute, 35
Who taught thee to eat bread fit for divinity,
To drink wine fit for royalty,

Who clothed thee with a magnificent garment,
And who gave thee splendid Gilgamesh for thy companion?
And now, my friend, Gilgamesh, thine own brother,   40
[Lets] thee rest on a magnificent couch;
He lets thee rest [on] a couch of honor.
[He lets] thee sit on a seat of ease, the seat at (his) left,
[So that the prin]ces of the earth kiss thy feet.
Over thee [he will cause] the people of Uruk [to wee]p (and)
        to lament.   45
[The thriving] people he will burden with service for thee.
[And he himself], after thou (art buried), will cause [his] body
        to wear long hair.
[He will clothe himself] with the skin of a lion and will roam
        over the d[esert]."
[When] Enkidu [heard] the words of valiant Shamash,
[. . .] his angry heart grew quiet.   50

About two lines wanting. Enkidu relents and turns the curse into
a blessing.

Tablet VII/Column iv

.   .   .   .
"[Kings, prin]ces, and grandees shall love [thee].
[. . . s]mite his thigh.
[. . . shall] shake the hair of his head.
[. . . the . . .] . . . shall unloose his girdle for thee.   5
[. . .] basalt(?), lapis lazuli, and gold.
] . . . [. . . .
[For thee . . .] . . . his storehouses are filled.
[Before] the gods [the priest] shall lead thee.
[On account of thee(?)] the wife, the mother of seven, shall be
        forsaken."   10
[. . . Enki]du, whose body is sick.
[. . .] he sleeps alone.
[. . .]during the night [he pours out] his heart to his friend.
"[My friend], I saw a dream this night.
The heavens [roared], the earth resounded.[45]   15

45. This is a portent of death.

[. . .] I was standing(?) by myself.

[. . . appeared], somber was his face.

His face was like [that of Zû(?)].

[. . .] his talons were (like) the talons of an eagle.

[. . .] he overpowered(?) me.   20

[. . .] . . . he leaps.

[. . .] submerged me.

(Break)

[. . .] . . . he transformed me,

[That] mine arms [were covered with feathers] like a bird.

He looks at me (and) leads me to the house of darkness, to the
    dwelling of Irkalla;[46]

To the house from which he who enters never goes forth;

On the road whose path does not lead back;   35

To the house whose occupants are bereft of light;

Where dust is their food and clay their sustenance;

(Where) they are clad like birds, with garments of wings;

(Where) they see no light and dwell in darkness.

In the h[ouse of dus]t, which I entered,   40

I loo[ked at the kings(?)], and (behold!) the crowns had been
    deposited.

. . . [. . .] those who (used to wear) crowns, who from the
    days of old had ruled the land,

[The representatives(?)] of Anu and Enlil, (it was) they who
    served the fried meat,

Who served the [baked goods], who served cold water from the
    skins.

In the house of dust, which I entered,   45

Dwell high priest and acolyte;

There dwell incantation priest and ecstatic;

There dwell the attendants of the lavers of the great gods;

There dwells Etana,[47] there dwells Sumuqan;

[There also dwells] Ereshkigal, the queen of the underworld.   50

[Bêlit]-sêri, the scribe of the underworld, kneels before her.

[She holds a tablet(?)] and reads before her.

46. The queen of the underworld.
47. A king of Kish, said to have been carried to heaven by an eagle.

[She lifted] her head (and) saw me.
[. . .] and she took that [man][48] away."

Here follows a gap of about fifty-five lines. The following fragment contains a speech by Gilgamesh, presumably addressed to his mother.

"[My] friend saw a dream with ominous [meaning . . .].   5
The day on which he saw the dream was ended [. . .].
Enkidu lay stricken, one day [. . .],
Which Enkidu on his couch [. . .].
A third day and a fourth day [. . .];
A fifth, a sixth, a seventh, an eighth, a ninth, [and a tenth
    day].   10
Enkidu's illness [grew worse and worse].
An eleventh and a twelfth day [. . .].
Enkidu [lay] upon [his] couch [. . .].
He called Gilgamesh [. . .]:
'[My] friend, [. . .] has cursed me.   15
[I shall not die] like one who [falls] in [battle].
I was afraid of the battle and [. . .].
My friend, he who [falls] in bat[tle is blessed(?)],
(But) I, [I shall die in disgrace(?)].' "

(Break)

Tablet VIII/Column i

[As soon as] the first shimmer of [morning beamed forth],[49]
Gilga[mesh opened his mouth and said to] his [friend]:
"O En[kidu, . . . like(?)] a gazelle;
And it was thou [whom . . .];
It was thou whom the [. . .] reared.   5
And [. . .] the pasture.
Moun[tains we ascended(?) and went down(?) to] the cedar
    forest."

In the next fourteen lines, too fragmentary for translation, Gilgamesh apparently continues the recital of the valiant deeds which

48. Enkidu means himself.
49. Here the translator has improved upon the original "something of
(morning)."

the two heroes performed together. After that the text breaks off. Gilgamesh is steeped in sorrow at the death of his friend and turns to the elders of the city with these plaintive words:

Tablet VIII/Column ii

"Hearken unto me, O elders, [and give ear] unto me!
It is for Enk[idu], my [friend], that I weep,
Crying bitterly like unto a wailing woman.
The hatchet at my side, [the bo]w in my hand,
The dagger in my belt, [the shield] that was before me,   5
My festal attire, my [only(?)] joy!
An evil [foe(?)] arose and [robbed(?)] me.
[My friend], my [younger broth]er(?), who chased the wild
    ass of the open country (and) the panther of the steppe;
E[nkidu], my friend, my younger brother(?), who chased the
    wild ass of the open country (and) the panther of the steppe.
We who [conquered] all (difficulties), who ascended [the
    mountains];   10
Who seized and [killed] the bull of heaven;
Who overthrew Hubaba,[50] that [dwelt] in the [cedar] forest—!
Now what sleep is this that has taken hold of [thee]?
Thou hast become dark and canst not hear [me]."
But he does not lift [his eyes].   15
He touched his heart, but it did not beat.
Then he veiled (his) friend like a bride [. . .].
He lifted [his voice] like a lion,
Like a lioness robbed of [her] whelps
He went back and forth before [his friend],   20
Pulling out (his hair) and throwing (it) away [. . .],[51]
Taking off and throwing down (his) beautiful (clothes) [. . .].
[As soon as] the first shimmer of [morning] beamed forth, Gil-
    [gamesh . . .].

(Break)

50. Variant form of Humbaba or Huwawa.
51. Compare Jeremiah 7:29: "Cut off thine hair, O Jerusalem, and cast it away, and take up a lamentation on high places. . . ."

Tablet VIII/Column iii

"On a couch [of honor I let thee recline].
I let thee sit [on a seat of ease, the seat at my left],
So that the princes of the earth [kissed thy feet].
Over thee I will cause the people [of Uruk] to weep [and to lament].
The thriving people [I will burden with service for thee].   5
And I myself, after thou (art buried), [will cause my body to wear long hair].
I will clothe myself with the skin of a l[ion and will roam over the desert]."
As soon as the first shimmer of morning be[amed forth, Gilgamesh . . .].
He loosened his girdle [. . .].

From here to column v, line 42, hardly anything has been preserved. The missing portion probably dealt with the burial of Enkidu.

Tablet VIII/Column v

[. . .] judge of the Anunna[ki . . .].
When [Gilga]mesh heard this,
He conceived [in his heart] an image(?) of the river(?).
As soon as the first shimmer of morning beamed forth, Gilgamesh fashioned [. . .].   45
He brought out a large table of *elammaqu*-wood.
A bowl of carnelian(?) he filled with honey.
A bowl of lapis lazuli he filled with butter.
[. . .] he adorned and exposed to the sun.

With the exception of about four signs, column vi has been completely destroyed.

Tablet IX/Column i

Gilgamesh for Enkidu, his friend,
Weeps bitterly and roams over the desert.
"When I die, shall I not be like unto Enkidu?
Sorrow has entered my heart.

I am afraid of death and roam over the desert.   5
To Utnapishtim,[52] the son of Ubara-Tutu,
I have (therefore) taken the road and shall speedily go there.
When (on previous occasions) I arrived at mountain passes by
      night,
(And) saw lions and was afraid,
I lifted my head to Sin[53] (and) prayed;   10
To the [light(?)] of the gods my prayers ascended.
[Also now, O Sin], preserve me!"
[During the night he] lay down and awoke from a dream:
[. . .] they were rejoicing in life.
He took [his] hatchet in his hand.   15
He drew [the sword] from his belt.
Like an ar[row(?)] he fell among them.
He smote [. . .] and broke (them) to pieces.

(Lines 19-28 are too fragmentary for translation.)
(Remainder broken away. Gilgamesh arrives at a mountain range.)

Tablet IX/Column ii

The name of the mountain is Mâshu.[54]
As he arri[ves] at the mountain of Mâshu,
Which every day keeps watch over the rising [and setting of
      the sun],
Whose peak(s) r[each] (as high as) the "banks of heaven,"
(And) whose breast reaches down to the underworld,   5
The scorpion-people keep watch at its gate,
Those whose radiance is terrifying and whose look is death,
Whose frightful splendor overwhelms mountains,
Who at the rising and setting of the sun keep watch over the sun.
When Gilgamesh saw them,   10
His face became gloomy with fear and dismay.
(But) he collected his thoughts[55] and bowed down before them.
The scorpion-man calls to his wife:

52. The Babylonian Noah.
53. The moon god.
54. If this name is Babylonian, it means "Twins." In the text it is treated
as either singular or plural.
55. Literally, "seized his sense."

"He who has come to us, his body is the flesh of gods!"
The wife of the scorpion-man answers him: 15
"Two-(thirds) of him is god, one-third of him is man."
The sco[rpion-m]an calls the man,
Speaking (these) words [to the offspri]ng of the gods:
"[Why hast thou traveled such] a long journey?
[Why hast thou come all the way] to me,   20
[Crossing seas] whose crossings are difficult?
[The purpose of] thy [comi]ng I should like to learn."

(Remainder broken away)

Tablet IX/Column iii

(Lines 1-2 are destroyed.)

"[For the sake of] Utnapishtim, my father, [have I come],
Who entered into the assembly of [the gods . . .].
Concerning life and death [I would ask him]."   5
The scorpion-man opened his mouth [and said],
Speaking to [Gilgamesh]:
"There has not (yet) been anyone, Gilgamesh, [who has been
     able to do that].
No one has (yet) [traveled] the paths of the mountains.
At twelve double-hours the heart [. . .].   10
Dense is the darkness and [there is] no [light].
To the rising of the sun [. . .].
To the setting of the sun [. . .].
To the setting of [the sun . . .]."

(Lines 15-20 are badly damaged.)

(Remainder broken away)

Tablet IX/Column iv

(Top broken off)

"[Though it be] in sorrow [and pain],
In cold and [heat],
In sighing [and weeping, I will go]!   35
[Open] now [the gate of the mountains]."

The scorpion-man [opened his mouth and said]
To Gilgamesh [. . .]:
"Go, Gilga[mesh, . . .].
The mountains of Mâshu [I permit thee to cross];   40
The mountains (and) mounta[in ranges thou mayest traverse].
Safely may [thy feet carry thee back].
The gate of the mountain(s) [is open to thee]."
[When] Gilga[mesh heard this],
[He followed(?)] the word of [the scorpion-man].   45
Along the road of the sun [he went(?)]⁵⁶
One double-hour [he traveled];
Dense is the dark[ness and there is no light];
Neither [what lies ahead of him nor what lies behind him] does
    it per[mit him to see].⁵⁷
Two double-hours [he traveled].   50

Tablet IX/Column v

(Top broken off)

Four [double-hours he traveled];
Dense [is the darkness and there is no light];
Neither [what lies ahead of him nor what lies behind him] does
    it per[mit him to see].   25
Five double-hours [he traveled];
Dense is the da[rkness and there is no light];
Neither [what lies ahead of him nor what lies behind him] does
    it permit [him to see].
[Six double-hours he traveled];
Dense is the darkness a[nd there is no light];   30
Neither [what lies ahead of him nor what lies behind him] does
    it permit [him to see].
After he has traveled seven double-hours [. . .];
Dense is the darkness and [there is] no [light];
Neither what lies [ahe]ad of him nor what lies behind [him]
    does it permit him [to see].
Eight double-hours [he traveled, and] he cries out(?);   35

56. Apparently from east to west.
57. Literally, "It does not permit him to see his front nor his rear."

Dense is the dar[kness and] there is [no] light;
Neither what lies [ahead] of him nor what lies behind him does
    it per[mit him to see].
Nine double-[hours he traveled, and he feels(?)] the north wind.
[. . .] his face.
[(But) dense is the darkness and there is no] light;   40
[Neither what lies ahea]d of him nor what lies behind him
    [does it permit him to see].
[After] he [has trave]led [ten double-hours],
[. . .] is close.
[. . .] of the double-hour.
[After he has traveled eleven double-hours he co]mes out before
    sun(rise).   45
[After he has traveled twelve double-hours], it is light.
Be[fore him stand] shrubs of (precious) [stone]s; as he sees
    (them) he draws nigh.
The carnelian bears its fruit;
Vines hang from it, good to look at.
The lapis lazuli bears . . . ;   50
Also fruit it bears, pleasant to behold.

Tablet IX/Column vi

(Top broken away)

Lines 24-36 are too fragmentary for translation. Enough is left,
however, to show that they continue the description of the mar-
velous garden of precious stones.

Sid[uri,[58] the barmaid], who dwells by the edge of the sea.

(Colophon:)

Ta[blet IX] of "He who saw everything," of the series of
    Gi[lgamesh].
Palace of Ashurbanipal,
King of the world, king of Assyria.   40

58. The name of the barmaid, Siduri, means "young woman" in Hurrian
(a language related to Hittite) and is used to describe Hebat, a form of
Ishtar, in the Hurrian texts. This tends to substantiate the statement that
Gilgamesh traveled in a westerly direction.

Tablet X

A. THE OLD BABYLONIAN VERSION

Tablet X/Column i

(Top broken away)

". . . . .

With their skins [he clothes himself] (and) eats (their) flesh.
. . . Gilgamesh, which has never been,
[As long as(?)] my gale[59] drives the water."
Shamash felt distressed, he went to him, 5
(And) said to Gilgamesh:
"Gilgamesh, whither runnest thou?
The life which thou seekest thou wilt not find."
Gilgamesh said to him, to valiant Shamash:
"After walking (and) running over the steppe, 10
Shall I rest my head in the midst of the earth
That I may sleep all the years?
Let mine eyes see the sun that I may be sated with light.
(Banished) afar is the darkness, if the light is sufficient(?).
May he who has died the death see the light of the sun."[60] 15

Tablet X/Column ii

(The top is broken away. Gilgamesh is addressing Siduri, the bar-maid.)

"He who went with me through all hard[ships],
Enkidu, whom I loved (so) dearly,
Who went with me through all hardships,
He has gone to the (common) lot of mankind.
Day and night I have wept over him. 5
For burial I did not want to give him up, (thinking):
'My friend will rise after all at my lamentation!'
Seven days and seven nights,
Until the worm fell upon his face.

59. The gale of Siduri?
60. The translation of these last two lines is quite uncertain.

Since he is gone, I find no life.   10
I have roamed about like a hunter in the midst of the steppe.
(And) now, O barmaid, that I see thy face,
May I not see death, which I dread!"
The barmaid said to him, to Gilgamesh:

Tablet X/Column iii

"Gilgamesh, whither runnest thou?
The life which thou seekest thou wilt not find;
(For) when the gods created mankind,
They allotted death to mankind,
(But) life they retained in their keeping.   5
Thou, O Gilgamesh, let thy belly be full;
Day and night be thou merry;
Make every day (a day of) rejoicing.
Day and night do thou dance and play.
Let thy raiment be clean,   10
Thy head be washed, (and) thyself be bathed in water.
Cherish the little one holding thy hand,
(And) let the wife rejoice in thy bosom.
This is the lot of [mankind . . .]."

(Remainder broken away)

Tablet X/Column iv

In his wrath he destroys them.[61]
He returns and steps up to him.[62]
His eyes behold Sursunabu.
Sursunabu says to him, to Gilgamesh:
"Tell me, what is thy name?   5
I am Sursunabu, belonging to Utanapishtim[63] the Distant."

61. The stone images. Compare Tablet X, ii, 29 and iii, 38 (Assyrian Version).
62. Sursunabu. Sursunabu was the boatman of Utnapishtim. In the Assyrian recension the boatman is called Urshanabi.
63. Assyrian for Utnapishtim. It may mean "I have found life," in contrast to the "life thou shalt not find" (X, i, 8 and iii, 2 of the Old Babylonian Version) with which Gilgamesh is confronted.

Gilgamesh said to him, to Sursunabu:
"Gilgamesh is my name,
Who have come from Uruk, the house of Anu,
Who have traversed the mountains,   10
A long journey, (from) the rising of the sun.
Now that I see thy face, Sursunabu,
Show me [Utanapishtim] the Distant."
Sursunabu [said] to him, to Gilgamesh:

(Remainder lost)

B.   THE ASSYRIAN VERSION

Tablet X/Column i

Siduri, the barm[aid, who dwells by the edge of the sea],
(Who) dwells [. . .],
For her they made a jug, for her they made a golden mashing-
        vat.
She is covered with a veil and [. . .].
Gilgamesh comes along and [. . .].   5
He is clad in pelts, [. . .].
He has the flesh of gods in [his body],
(But) there is woe in [his heart].
[His] face [is like] unto (that of) one who has made a far
        journey.
The barmaid looks [out] into the distance;   10
She says to her heart (and) [speaks] (these) words,
[As she takes counsel] with herself:
"Surely, this (man) is a murder[er]!
Whither is he bound . . . [. . .]?"
When the barmaid saw him, she barred [her door],   15
She barred her gate, barring it [with a crossbar].
But he, Gilgamesh, heard [the sound of her shutting(?)].
He lifted his chin and pla[ced(?) . . .].
Gilgamesh [said] to her, [the barmaid]:
"Barmaid, what didst thou see [that thou hast barred thy door], 20
That thou hast barred thy gate, [barring it with a crossba]r?
I shall smash [thy] door [and bre]ak [thy gate]!"

The remainder of the column is broken away. But the greater part of it can be restored from another fragment and from the succeeding columns of this tablet.

[Gilgamesh said to her, to the barmaid]:
"[I am Gilgamesh; I seized and killed the bull which came
     down out of heaven];
[I killed the watchman of the forest];
[I overthrew Humbaba, who dwelt in] the ce[dar forest];
[In the mountain passes(?) I kil]led the lions."   5
[The barmaid sa]id [to him], to Gilgamesh:
"[If thou art Gilgamesh], who didst kill the watchman (of the
     forest);
[(If) thou didst overthrow Humb]aba, who dwelt in the cedar
     forest,
Kill the lions in the mountain [passes(?)],
[Seize and] kill the bull which came down out of heaven,   10
[Why are (thy) chee]ks (so) [emaciated], (and why) is thy
     face downcast?
[(Why) is thy heart (so) sad], (and why) are thy features
     (so) [distor]ted?
[(Why) is there woe] in thy heart,
(And why is) thy face [unto (that of) one who has made a far
     journey]?
[(Why) . . .] is thy countenance burned [with cold and
     heat]?   15
[(And why . . .] dost thou roam over the steppe?"
[Gilgamesh said to her, to the barmaid]:
"[Barmaid, should not my cheeks be emaciated (and) my face
     be downcast]?
[Should not my heart be sad (and) my features be distorted]?
[Should there not be woe in my heart]?   20
[Should my face not be like unto (that of) one who has made a
     far journey]?
[Should my countenance not be burned with cold and heat]?
[And should . . . I not roam over the steppe]?
[My friend, my younger brother(?), who chased the wild ass of
     the open country (and) the panther of the steppe],

[Enkidu, my friend, my younger brother(?), who chased the
    wild ass of the open country (and) the panther of the
    steppe]!   25
[We who conquered all difficulties and ascended the mountains],

Tablet X/Column ii

[Who seized and killed the bull of heaven],
[Who overthrew Humbaba, that dwelt in the cedar forest]!
[My friend, whom I loved (so) dearly, who went with me
    through all hardships];
[Enkidu, my friend, whom I loved (so) dearly, who went with
    me through all hardships],
[Him the fate of mankind has overtaken]!   5
[Six days and seven nights I wept over him].
[Until the worm fell upon his face].
[I became afraid of death, so that I now roam over the steppe].
    The matter of my friend [rests heavy upon me],
[Hence far and wide I roam over the ste]ppe; the matter of
    Enkidu, [my friend, rests heavy upon me],
[Hence far and wide] I roam over [the steppe].   10
[How can I be sile]nt? How can I be quiet?
[My friend, whom I loved, has turn]ed to clay; Enkidu, my
    friend, whom I loved, has tu[rned to clay].
[And I], shall I [not like unto him] lie down
[And not rise] forever?"
[Gilgamesh furthermore] said to her, to the barmaid: 15
"[Now], barmaid, which is the way to Utnapi[shtim]?
[What are] the directions? Give me, oh, give me the directions![64]
If it is possible, (even) the sea will I cross!
(But) if it is not possible, I will roam over the steppe."
The barmaid said to him, to Gilgamesh: 20
"Gilgamesh, there never has been a crossing;
And whoever from the days of old has come thus far has not
    been able to cross the sea.
Valiant Shamash does cross the sea, (but) who besides Shamash
    crosses (it)?

64. Literally, "[What is] its mark? Give me, oh, give me its mark!"

Difficult is the place of crossing (and) very difficult its passage;

And deep are the waters of death, which bar its approaches.   25

Where, Gilgamesh, wilt thou cross the sea?

(And) when thou arrivest at the waters of death, what wilt thou do?

Gilgamesh, there is Urshanabi,[65] the boatman of Utnapishtim.

With him are the stone images(?);[66] in the woods he picks . . .

[Hi]m let thy face behold.   30

[If it is possi]ble, cross over with him; if it is not possible, turn back (home)."

When [Gilgam]esh heard this,

[He took (his) hat]chet in hi[s hand];

[He drew the dagger from his belt], slipped into (the woods), and went down to them.[67]

[Like an arrow(?) he f]ell among them.   35

(Lines 36-50 are too fragmentary for translation.)

Tablet X/Column iii

Urshanabi said to him, to Gi[lgamesh]:

"Why are thy cheeks (so) emaciated, (and why) [is thy face] dow[ncast]?

(Why) is thy heart (so) sad, [and (why) are thy features (so) distorted]?

(Why) is there woe in [thy heart]?

(Why) [is thy face like unto] (that of) one who has made a far journey?   5

(Why) [is thy countenance bur]ned with cold and heat?

(And why) [. . .] dost thou [roam over the steppe]?"

[Gilgamesh] said [to him], to [Urshanabi]:

"[Urshanabi, should not my ch]eeks [be emaciated (and) my face be downcast]?

[Should not] my [hea]rt [be sad] (and) [my features] be distorted?   10

65. Assyrian equivalent of the Babylonian Sursunabu.
66. Literally, "those of stones." The Hittite version has: "two images of stone." These images may perhaps have been idols enabling Urshanabi to cross the waters of death.
67. To the stone images?

[Should there not be] woe in [my heart]?

[Should my] fa[ce not be like unto (that of) one who has made a far journey]?

[Should my countenance] not be bu[rned with cold and heat]?

[(And) should . . . I not roam over the steppe]?

[My friend, my younger brother(?), who chased the wild ass of the open country (and) the panther of the steppe],   15

[Enkidu, my friend, my younger brother(?), who chased the wild ass of the open country (and) the panther of the steppe]!

[We who conquered all (difficulties) and ascended the mountains],

[Who seized and killed the bull of heaven],

[Who overthrew Humbaba, that dwelt in the cedar forest]!

My friend, [whom I loved (so) dearly, who went with me through all hardships],   20

Enk[idu, my friend, whom I loved (so) dearly, who went with me through all hardships],

[Him the fate of mankind] has overtaken!

Six days [and seven nights I wept over him],

Until [the worm fell upon his face].

I became frighte[ned . . . and became afraid of death, so that I now roam over the steppe].   25

The matt[er of my friend rests heavy upon me],

Hence far and wide[68] I [roam over the steppe; the matter of Enkidu, my friend, rests heavy upon me],

[Hence] far and wide [I roam over the steppe].

How can I be sil[ent? How can I be quiet]?

My friend, whom I loved, has tur[ned to clay].   30

(And) I, shall I not like unto him lie [down and not rise forever]?"

Gilgamesh (furthermore) said to him, to [Urshanabi]:

"Now, Urshanabi, which [is the road to Utnapishtim]?

What are the directions? Give me, oh, give [me the directions]!

If it is possible, (even) the sea will I cross; (but) if it is not possible, [I will roam over the steppe]."   35

---

68. Literally, "a long road."

Urshanabi said to him, to [Gilgamesh]:

"Thy hands, O Gilgamesh, have prevented [thy crossing the sea];

(For) thou hast destroyed the stone images(?) . . . .

The stone images(?) are destroyed . . . .

Take the hatchet in [thy hand], O Gilgamesh.   40

Go down to the forest and [cut one hundred and twenty] punting-poles, each sixty cubits (in length).

Put bitumen[69] and plates(?)[70] (on them and) bring [them to me]."

When Gilgamesh [heard] this,

He took the hatchet in his hand, he d[rew the sword from his belt],

He went down to the forest and [cut one hundred and twenty] punting-poles, each sixty cubits (in length).   45

He put bitumen and plates(?) (on them) and brought (them) [to him].

Gilgamesh and Urshanabi (then) boarded [the ship].

They launched the ship on the billows and [glided along].

On the third day their voyage was the same as (an ordinary one of) a month and fifteen days.

Thus Urshanabi arrived at the waters of [death].   50

Tablet X/Column iv

Urshanabi [said] to him, [to Gilgamesh]:

"Press on, Gilgamesh! [Take a pole (for thrusting) . . .].

Let not thy hand touch the waters of death [. . .].

Gilgamesh, take thou a second, a third, and a fourth pole;

Gilgamesh, take thou a fifth, a sixth, and a seventh pole;   5

Gilgamesh, take thou an eighth, a ninth, and a tenth pole;

Gilgamesh, take thou an eleventh, (and) a twelfth pole!"

With one hundred and twenty (thrusts) Gilgamesh had used up the poles.[71]

69. To judge from modern practice in Babylonia, this expression probably refers to the knobs of bitumen at the upper end of the punting-pole.

70. Probably some kind of plate or socket at the lower end of a punting pole.

71. Each pole was good for only one thrust, since after each push the pole was wet almost to its full length and could no longer be employed with both hands, lest they "touch the waters of death."

He ungirded his loins . . . [. . .].
Gilgamesh pulled off [his] clothes [. . .].   10
With his hands he raised the mast(?).
Utnapishtim looks into the distance;
He says to his heart (and) [speaks] (these) words,
[As he takes counsel] with himself:
"Why are [the stone images(?)] of the ship destroyed?   15
And (why) does one who is not its master ride [upon it]?
The man who is coming there is none of mine . . . [. . .].
I look, but not [. . .].
I look, but not [. . .].
I look, but [. . .]."   20

The remainder of the column is broken away. Gilgamesh meets
Utnapishtim and is asked the same questions that were addressed
to him by the barmaid and the boatman. Gilgamesh answers Utnapishtim in exactly the same words.

[Gilgamesh said to him, to Utnapishtim]:
"[Utnapishtim, should not my cheeks be emaciated (and) my
      face be downcast]?

Tablet X/Column v

[Should not my heart be sad] (and) my fea[tures be distorted]?
[Should there not be woe in] my [he]art?
[Should] my [face] not be like [unto (that of) one who has
      made a far journey]?
[Should] my countenance [not be burned with heat and cold]?
[(And) should . . . I not] roam over the steppe?   5
[My friend, my younger brother(?), who chased the wild ass
      of the open country] (and) the panther of the steppe,
[Enkidu, my friend, my younger brother(?)], who chased the
      wild ass of the open country (and) the panther of the
      steppe!
[We who conquered all (difficulties) and ascended] the moun-
      tains,
[Who captured and] killed [the bull of] heaven,
[Who overthrew Humbaba, that] dwelt in the cedar forest!   10

[My friend, who kil]led [with me] the lions,
[My friend, who went with me through] all hardships,
[Enkidu, my friend, who] killed [with me] the lions,
[Him the fate of mankind has overtaken! Six days and seven
    nights] I wept over him,
For burial [I did not want to give him up],   15
[Until the worm fell upon] his [face].
[I became frightened . . . and] became afra[id of] death, [so
    that I now roam over the s]teppe.
[The matter of my friend rests] heavy upon me, so that far
    and wide [I roam over the ste]ppe;
[The matter of Enkidu], my friend, rests heavy upon me, so
    that far and wide [I roam over the steppe].
[How] can I be silent? How can I be quiet?   20
[My friend, wh]om I loved, has turned to clay; Enkidu [my]
    friend, [whom I loved, has turned to clay].
[(And) I], shall I not like unto him lie down and not rise for-
    ever?"
Gilgamesh (furthermore) said to him, to Utnapi[shtim]:
"That [no]w I might come and see Utnapishtim, whom they
    call 'the Distant,'
[I] went roaming around over all the lands,   25
I crossed many difficult mountains,
I crossed all the seas;
Of sweet sleep my face has not had its fill;
[I] have wearied myself with walking around (and) have filled
    my joints with woe.
Not (yet) had I come [to the ho]use of the barmaid when my
    clothing was worn out.   30
[I kille]d bear, hyena, lion, panther, tiger, stag, ibex, wild
    game, and the creatures of the steppe;
Their [flesh] I ate (and) their pelts I pu[t on(?)].
[. . .]let them bar her gate, with pitch and bitu[men . . .]."

(Lines 34-5 are too fragmentary for translation.)

[Utnapishtim] said to him, to [Gilgamesh]:

(Lines 37-50 are too fragmentary for translation.)

Tablet X/Column vi

(Top broken away)

"Do we build a house (to stand) forever? Do we seal (a docu-
      ment to be in force) forever?
Do brothers divide (their inheritance to last) forever?
Does hatred remain in [the land] forever?
Does the river raise (and) ca[rry] the flood forever?
. . . .   30

Does its face see the face of the sun (forever)?
From the days of old there is no [permanence].
The sleeping(?) and the dead, how alike [they are]!
Do they not (both) draw the picture of death?
. . . [. . .]   35
The Anunnaki, the great gods, ga[ther together];
Mammetum, the creatress of destiny, de[crees] with them the
      destinies.
Life and death they allot;
The days of death they do not reveal."
Gilgamesh said to him to Utnapishtim the Distant: 40

(Colophon:)

Tablet X of "He who saw everything," of the series of Gilga-
      mesh.
Palace of Ashurbanipal, king of the world, king of Assyria.

Tablet XI

Gilgamesh said to him, to Utnapishtim the Distant:
"I look upon thee, Utnapishtim,
Thine appearance is not different; thou art like unto me.
Yea, thou art not different; thou art like unto me.
My heart had pictured thee as one perfect for the doing of
      battle;   5
[But] thou liest (idly) on (thy) side, (or) on thy back.
[Tell me], how didst thou enter into the company of the gods
      and obtain life (everlasting)?"

Utnapishtim said to him, to Gilgamesh:
"Gilgamesh, I will reveal unto thee a hidden thing,
Namely, a secret of the gods will I tell thee.   10
Shurippak[72]—a city which thou knowest,
[And which] is situated [on the bank of] the river Euphrates—
That city was (already) old, and the gods were in its midst.
(Now) their heart prompted the great gods [to] bring a deluge.
[There was(?)] Anu, their father;   15
Warlike Enlil, their counselor;
Ninurta, their representative;
Ennugi, their vizier;
Ninigiku, (that is) Ea, also sat with them.
Their speech he repeated to a reed hut:[73]   20
'Reed hut, reed hut! Wall, wall!
Reed hut, hearken! Wall, consider!
Man of Shurippak,[74] son of Ubara-Tutu!
Tear down (thy) house, build a ship!
Abandon (thy) possessions, seek (to save) life!   25
Disregard (thy) goods, and save (thy) life!
[Cause to] go up into the ship the seed of all living creatures.
The ship which thou shalt build,
Its measurements shall be (accurately) measured;
Its width and its length shall be equal.   30
Cover it [li]ke the subterranean waters.'
When I understood this, I said to Ea, my lord:
'[Behold], my lord, what thou hast thus commanded,
[I] will honor (and) carry out.
[But what] shall I answer the city, the people, and the elders?' 35
Ea opened his mouth and said,
Speaking to me, his servant:
'Thus shalt thou say to them:
[I have le]arned that Enlil hates me,
That I may no (longer) dwell in yo[ur ci]ty,   40
Nor turn my face to the land of Enlil.

72. Variant spelling for Shuruppak, a city of central Sumer.
73. Probably the dwelling of Utnapishtim.
74. As shown by the following lines, this expression refers to Utnapishtim.

[I will therefore g]o down to the *apsû* and dwell with Ea, my
    [lor]d.[75]
[On] you he will (then) rain down plenty;
[. . . of b]irds(?), . . . of fishes.
[. . .] harvest-wealth.   45
[In the evening the leader] of the storm(?)
Will cause a wheat-rain to rain down upon you.'[76]
As soon as [the first shimmer of mor]ning beamed forth,
The land was gathered [about me].

(Lines 50-53 are too fragmentary for translation.)

The child [brou]ght pitch,
(While) the strong brought [whatever else] was needful.   55
On the fifth day [I] laid its framework.
One *ikû*[77] was its floor space, one hundred and twenty cubits
    each was the height of its walls;
One hundred and twenty cubits measured each side of its deck.[78]
I 'laid the shape' of the outside (and) fashioned it.[79]
Six (lower) decks I built into it,   60
(Thus) dividing (it) into seven (stories).
Its ground plan I divided into nine (sections).[80]
I drove water-stoppers into it.[81]

---

75. The *apsû*, the place where Ea had his dwelling, was the subterranean
sweet-water ocean, from which the water of rivers, marshes, etc. was
thought to spring forth. But here, in view of all the things Utnapishtim
takes along, the reference probably is to the marshy area at the northern
shores of the Persian Gulf.
76. Here the original obviously has a play on words, the purpose of which
is to deceive the inhabitants of Shurippak until the last moment. This line
can also be translated: "He will cause a destructive rain (lit.: a rain of
misfortune) to rain down upon you." This evidently is the real meaning of
the passage. But Ea knew that the people of Shurippak would interpret
these words differently.
77. About 3,600 square meters, or approximately an acre.
78. Placing the Babylonian cubit at about half a meter, the deck had a sur-
face of approximately 3,600 meters, or one *ikû*. Utnapishtim's boat was an
exact cube.
79. The ship. Utnapishtim now attached the planking to the framework.
80. Each of the seven stories was divided into nine sections, or compart-
ments.
81. This line probably means that he drove wedge-shaped pieces of wood
between the seams to help make the boat watertight.

I provided punting-poles and stored up a supply.[82]

Six *shar*[83] of pitch I poured into the furnace,   65

(And) three *shar* of asphalt [I poured] into it.

Three *shar* of oil the basket-carriers brought:[84]

Besides a *shar* of oil which the saturation(?) (of the water-
     stoppers) consumed,

Two *shar* of oil [which] the boatman stowed away.

Bullocks I slaughtered for [the people];   70

Sheep I killed every day.

Must, red wine, oil, and white wine,

[I gave] the workmen [to drink] as if it were river water,

(So that) they made a feast as on New Year's Day.

I [. . .] ointment I put my hands.   75

[. . .] . . . the ship was completed.

Difficult was [the . . .].

. . . above and below.

[. . .] . . . its two-thirds.

[Whatever I had I] loaded aboard her.   80

Whatever I had of silver I loaded aboard her;

Whatever I [had] of gold I loaded aboard her;

Whatever I had of the seed of all living creatures [I loaded]
     aboard her.

After I had caused all my family and relations to go up into
     the ship,

I caused the game of the field, the beasts of the field, (and) all
     the craftsmen to go (into it).   85

Shamash set for me a definite time:

'When the leader of the sto[rm(?)] causes a destructive rain to
     rain down in the evening,

Enter the ship and close thy door.'

82. Or: what was needful (cf. line 55).

83. Var.: three *shar*. One *shar* is 3,600. The measure is not given in these lines. Perhaps we have to supply *sûtû*; one *sûtû* was equal to a little over two gallons. Three *shar* would then correspond to about 24,000 gallons.

84. If the translation "basket-carriers" is correct, we may perhaps assume that the baskets were coated with asphalt, or some such substance. But perhaps the oil was contained in vessels carried in some kind of slings. This latter mode of transportation is depicted on a plaque discovered among the ruins of Opis in Babylonia.

That definite time arrived:
In the evening the leader of the sto[rm(?)] caused a destructive
    rain to rain down.   90
I viewed the appearance of the weather;
The weather was frightful to behold.
I entered the ship and closed my door.
For the navigation(?) of the ship to the boatman Puzur-Amurri
I intrusted the mighty structure with its goods.   95
As soon as the first shimmer of morning beamed forth,
A black cloud came up from out the horizon.
Adad[85] thunders within it,
While Shullat and Hanish go before,
Coming as heralds over hill and plain;   100
Irragal[86] pulls out the masts;
Ninurta[87] comes along (and) causes the dikes to give way;
The Anunnaki[88] raised (their) torches,
Lighting up the land with their brightness;[89]
The raging of Adad reached unto heaven   105
(And) turned into darkness all that was light.
[. . .] the land he broke(?) like a po[t(?)].
(For) one day the tem[pest blew].
Fast it blew and [. . .].
Like a battle [it ca]me over the p[eople].   110
No man could see his fellow.
The people could not be recognized from heaven.
(Even) the gods were terror-stricken at the deluge.
They fled (and) ascended to the heaven of Anu;[90]
The gods cowered like dogs (and) crouched in distress(?).   115
Ishtar cried out like a woman in travail;
The lovely-voiced Lady of the g[ods] lamented:
'In truth, the olden time has turned to clay,

85. The god of storm and rain.
86. Another name for Nergal, the god of the underworld.
87. God of war and lord of the wells and irrigation works.
88. The judges in the underworld.
89. These two lines perhaps refer to sheet lightning on the horizon; forked
lightning, which is accompanied by thunder peals, is attributed to Adad.
90. Anu was the sky-god. The heaven of Anu was the highest of several
heavens in the Mesopotamian view of the universe.

Because I commanded evil in the assembly of the gods!
How could I command (such) evil in the assembly of the gods! 120
(How) could I command war to destroy my people,
(For) it is I who bring forth[91] (these) my people!
Like the spawn of fish they (now) fill the sea!'
The Anunnaki-gods wept with her;
The gods sat bowed (and) weeping. 125
Covered were their lips. . . .
Six days and [six] nights
The wind blew, the downpour, the tempest, (and) the flo[od]
    overwhelmed the land.
When the seventh day arrived, the tempest, the flood,
Which had fought like an army, subsided in (its) onslaught. 130
The sea grew quiet, the storm abated, the flood ceased.
I opened a window, and light fell upon my face.
I looked upon the sea,[92] (all) was silence,
And all mankind had turned to clay;
The . . . was as level as a (flat) roof. 135
I bowed, sat down, and wept,
My tears running down over my face.
I looked in (all) directions for the boundaries of the sea.
At (a distance of) twelve[93] (double-hours) there emerged a
    stretch of land.
On Mount Nisir the ship landed. 140
Mount Nisir held the ship fast and did not let (it) move.
One day, a second day Mount Nisir held the ship fast and did
    not let (it) move.
A third day, a fourth day Mount Nisir held the ship fast and
    did not let (it) move.
A fifth day, a sixth day Mount Nisir held the ship fast and did
    not let (it) move.[94]
When the seventh day arrived, 145

91. Literally, "give birth to."
92. Var.: at the weather.
93. Var.: fourteen.
94. In place of the words "held the ship fast and did not let (it) move," in lines 142-4, the original has the sign of reduplication or repetition, which means that the statement is to be completed on the basis of the preceding line.

I sent forth a dove and let (her) go.
The dove went away and came back to me;
There was no resting-place, and so she returned.
(Then) I sent forth a swallow and let (her) go.
The swallow went away and came back to me;   150
There was no resting-place, and so she returned.
(Then) I sent forth a raven and let (her) go.
The raven went away, and when she saw that the waters had
   abated,
She ate, she flew about, she cawed, (and) did not return.
(Then) I sent forth (everything) to the four winds and offered
   a sacrifice.   155
I poured out a libation on the peak of the mountain.
Seven and (yet) seven kettles I set up.
Under them I heaped up (sweet) cane, cedar, and myrtle.
The gods smelled the savor,
The gods smelled the sweet savor.   160
The gods gathered like flies over the sacrificer.
As soon as the great goddess[95] arrived,
She lifted up the great jewels which Anu had made according
   to her wish:
'O ye gods here present, as surely as I shall not forget the lapis
   lazuli on my neck,
I shall remember these days and shall not forget (them) ever!   165
Let the gods come near to the offering;
(But) Enlil shall not come near to the offering,
Because without reflection he brought on the deluge
And consigned my people to destruction!'
As soon as Enlil arrived   170
And saw the ship, Enlil was wroth;
He was filled with anger against the gods, the Igigi:[96]
'Has any of the mortals escaped? No man was to live through
   the destruction!'
Ninurta opened his mouth and said, speaking to warrior
   Enl[il]:
'Who can do things without Ea?   175

95. I.e., Ishtar.
96. The gods of heaven.

For Ea alone understands every matter.'

Ea opened his mouth and said, speaking to warrior Enlil:

'O warrior, thou wisest among the gods!

How, O how couldst thou without reflection bring on (this) deluge?

On the sinner lay his sin; on the transgressor lay his transgression!   180

Let loose, that he shall not be cut off; pull tight, that he may not ge[t (too) loose]⁹⁷

Instead of thy sending a deluge, would that a lion had come and diminished mankind!

(Or) instead of thy sending a deluge, would that a wolf had come and dim[inished] mankind!

(Or) instead of thy sending a deluge, would that a famine had occurred and [destroyed] the land!

(Or) instead of thy sending a deluge, would that Irra⁹⁸ had come and smitten mankind!   185

(Moreover,) it was not I who revealed the secret of the great gods;

(But) to Atrahasis⁹⁹ I showed a dream, and so he learned the secret of the gods.

And now take counsel concerning him.

Then Enlil went up into the ship.

He took my hand and caused me to go aboard.   190

He caused my wife to go aboard (and) to kneel down at my side.

Standing between us, he touched our foreheads and blessed us:

'Hitherto Utnapishtim has been but a man;

But now Utnapishtim and his wife shall be like unto us gods.

In the distance, at the mouth of the rivers, Utnapishtim shall dwell!'   195

So they took me and caused me to dwell in the distance, at the mouth of the rivers.

---

97. I.e., punish man, lest he get too wild; but do not be too severe, lest he perish.

98. The god of pestilence.

99. This name—in reality a descriptive epithet meaning "the exceedingly wise"—is another designation for Utnapishtim.

But now as for thee, who will assemble the gods unto thee,
That thou mayest find the life which thou seekest?
Come, do not sleep for six days and seven nights."
(But) as he sits (there) on his hams,   200
Sleep like a rainstorm blows upon him."
Utnapishtim says to her, to his wife:
"Look at the strong man who wants life (everlasting).
Sleep like a rainstorm blows upon him."
His wife says to him, to Utnapishtim the Distant: 205
"Touch him that the man may awake,
That he may return in peace on the road by which he came,
That through the gate through which he came he may return
    to his land."
Utnapishtim says to her, to his wife:
"Deceitful is mankind, he will try to deceive thee.[100]   210
Pray, (therefore,) bake loaves of bread for him (and) place
    (them) at his head.
And the days that he has slept mark on the wall!"
She baked loaves of bread for him (and) placed (them) at his
    head;
And the days that he slept she noted on the wall.
His first loaf of bread was all dried out;   215
The second was . . . ; the third was (still) moist; the fourth
    was white, his . . . ;
The fifth was moldy; the sixth had (just) been baked;
The seventh—suddenly he[101] touched him, and the man awoke.
Gilgamesh said to him, to Utnapishtim the Distant:
"Hardly did sleep spread over me,   220
When quickly thou didst touch me and rouse me."
Utnapishtim [said to him], to Gilgamesh:
"[. . . Gilga]mesh, count thy loaves of bread!
[The days which thou didst sleep] may they be known to thee.
Thy [first] loaf of bread [is(already) all dried out];   225
[The second is . . .]; the third is (still) moist; the fourth is
    white, thy . . . ;
[The fifth is mol]dy; the sixth has (just) been baked;

100. I.e., he will deny that he slept.
101. Utnapishtim.

[The seventh—s]uddenly thou didst wake."
[Gilg]amesh said to him, to Utnapishtim the Distant:
"[Oh, what] shall I do, Utnapishtim, (or) where shall I go,   230
As the robber[102] has (already) taken hold of my [member]s?
Death is dwelling [in] my bedchamber;
And wherever [I] set [my feet] there is death!"
Utnapishtim [said to him,] to Urshanabi, the boatman:
"Urshanabi, [may] the qua[y not re]joice in thee, may the
          place of crossing hate thee!   235
Him who walks about on its shore banish from its shore.
The man before whose face thou didst walk, whose body is
          covered with long hair,
The grace of whose members pelts have distorted,
Take him, Urshanabi, and bring him to the place of washing;
Let him wash his long hair (clean) as snow in water.   240
Let him throw off his pelts and let the sea carry (them) away,
          that his fair body may be seen.
Let the band around his head be replaced with a new one.
Let him be clad with a garment, as clothing for his nakedness.
Until he gets to his city,[103]
Until he finishes his journey,   245
May (his) garment not show (any sign of) age, but may it
          (still) be quite new."
Urshanabi took him and brought him to the place of washing.
He washed his long hair (clean) as snow in [water].
He threw off his pelts, that the sea might carry (them) away,
          (And that) his fair body appeared.   250
He rep[laced the band around] his head with a new one.
He clothed him with a garment, as clothing for his nakedness.
Until he [would come to his city],
Until he would finish his journey,
[(His) garment should not show (any sign of) age but] should
          (still) be quite new.   255
Gilgamesh and Urshanabi boarded the ship;
They launched the ship [on the billows] (and) glided along.
His wife said to him, to Utnapishtim the Distant:

102. I.e., death?
103. Var.: to his land.

"Gilgamesh has come hither, he has become weary, he has
    exerted himself,
What wilt thou give (him wherewith) he may return to his
    land?"   260
Then he, Gilgamesh, took a pole
And brought the ship near to the shore.[104]
Utnapishtim [said] to him, [to] Gilgamesh:
"Gilgamesh, thou hast come hither, thou hast become weary,
    thou hast exerted thyself;
What shall I give thee (wherewith) thou mayest return to thy
    land?   265
Gilgamesh, I will reveal (unto thee) a hidden thing,
Namely, a [secret of the gods will I] tell thee:
There is a plant like a thorn [. . .].
Like a rose(?) its thorn(s) will pr[ick thy hands].
If thy hands will obtain that plant, [thou wilt find new life]."   270
When Gilgamesh heard that, he opened [. . .].
He tied heavy stones [to his feet];
They pulled him down into the deep, [and he saw the plant].
He took the plant, (though) it pr[icked his hands].
He cut the heavy stones [from his feet],   275
(And) the . . . threw him to its shore.
Gilgamesh said to him, to Urshanabi, the boatman:
"Urshanabi, this plant is a wondrous(?) plant,
Whereby a man may obtain his former strength(?).
I will take it to Uruk, the enclosure, I will give (it) to eat
    [. . .]may cut off the plant(?).   280
Its name is 'The old man becomes young as the man (in his
    prime).'
I myself will eat (it) that I may return to my youth."[105]
After twenty double-hours they broke off a morsel.
After thirty (additional) double-hours they stopped for the
    night.

---

104. Gilgamesh was no doubt called back by Utnapishtim.
105. The purpose of this plant was to grant rejuvenated life; and it was to
be eaten after a person had reached old age. For this reason Gilgamesh
does not eat the plant at once but decides to wait until after his return to
Uruk, until he has become an "old man."

Gilgamesh saw a pool with cold water;   285
He descended into it and bathed in the water.
A serpent perceived the fragrance of the plant;
It came up [from the water] and snatched the plant,
Sloughing (its) skin on its return.[106]
Then Gilgamesh sat down (and) wept,   290
His tears flowing over his cheeks.
[. . .] of Urshanabi, the boatman:
"[For] whom, Urshanabi, have my hands become weary?
For whom is the blood of my heart being spent?
For myself I have not obtained any boon.   295
For the 'earth-lion'[107] have I obtained the boon.
Now at (a distance of) twenty[108] double-hours (such a) one(?)
        snatches it away (from me)!
When I opened the . . . .
I have found something that [has been s]et for a sign unto me;
        I will withdraw
And will leave the ship at the shore."[109] After twenty
        [double-hours] they broke off a morsel.   300
After thirty (additional) double-hours they stopped for the
        night. When they arrived in Uruk, the enclosure,
Gilgamesh said to him, to Urshanabi, the boatman:
"Urshanabi, climb upon the wall of Uruk (and) walk about;
Inspect the foundation terrace and examine the brickwork, if
        its brickwork be not of burnt bricks,
And (if) the seven wise men did not lay its foundation!   305
One shar[110] is city, one shar orchards, one shar prairie; (then
        there is) the uncultivated land(?) of the temple of Ishtar.
Three shar and the uncultivated land(?) comprise Uruk."

.   .   .   .

106. By eating this magic plant, the serpent gained the power to shed its
old skin and thereby to renew its life.
107. Apparently the serpent.
108. We should expect "fifty" (cf. lines 283-4).
109. In the loss of the plant Gilgamesh sees a sign that he should leave
the ship behind and proceed by land. The boatman goes along, for, according to line 235, he apparently has been banished from the shores of the
blessed for bringing Gilgamesh there.
110. Shar: 3,600. The measure is not given.

III

Egyptian Civilization

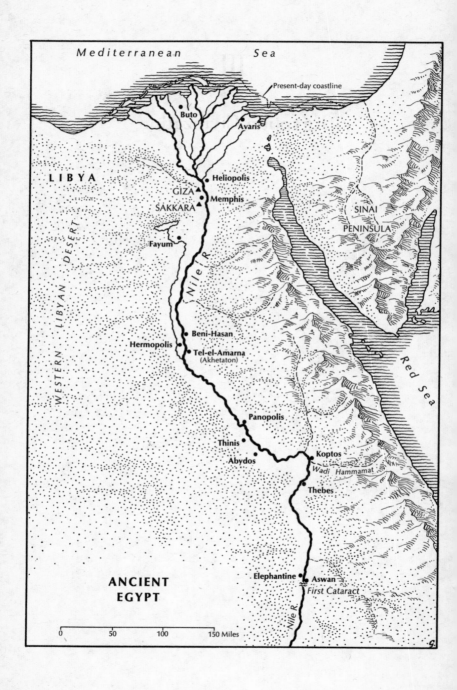

Mediterranean Sea

Present-day coastline

Buto

Avaris

LIBYA

Heliopolis

GIZA

Memphis

SAKKARA

SINAI
PENINSULA

Fayum

Nile R.

WESTERN LIBYAN DESERT

Beni-Hasan

Hermopolis

Tel-el-Amarna
(Akhetaton)

Red Sea

Panopolis

Thinis

Koptos

Abydos

Wadi Hammamat

Thebes

ANCIENT
EGYPT

Elephantine

Aswan
First Cataract

Nile R.

0   50   100   150 Miles

Introduction to The Pyramid Texts

The Pyramid Texts are among the oldest surviving examples of
Egyptian literature. They comprise a collection of funerary rites,
offerings, magical spells and incantations inscribed on the walls of
certain royal pyramids dating from the end of the Old Kingdom
and the beginning of the First Intermediate Period, *ca.* 2350-2150
B.C. The purpose of the texts was to guarantee the resurrection of
the Pharaoh after death, his successful journey to the afterworld,
and his immortality thereafter as one of the great gods, sometimes
as the greatest of all the gods.

These texts are for the most part incised in vertical columns on
the inside walls of the sarcophagus chamber, arranged in such a
way that the dead king in his coffin might see and read them.
Some, however, may be found on the walls of the antechamber, the
vestibule, or the passages between rooms. About seven thousand
lines of Pyramid Texts have been discovered to date, including
many repetitions of identical or virtually identical formulae.

Though written down mainly toward the end of the third millennium B.C., many of the Pyramid Texts are obviously much older.
Some of them no doubt existed in oral form before writing was developed. Certain passages must have originated at a time before the
union of Upper and Lower Egypt under Menes (*ca.* 3000 B.C.); for
they refer to hostilities between the North and South. Others obviously antedate the age of pyramid-building and mummification,
since they mention burying bodies in the sand. Scholars suppose
that utterances stressing the importance of the gods Horus and Set(h)
date from the Second Dynasty, when these gods were in favor in
royal circles; while formulae for the protection of pyramids must
have originated at a time subsequent to the construction of the first
of these great tombs.

At the time they were recorded on the pyramid walls, these
sacred texts were intended for the sole benefit of the Pharaoh: only
he could lay claim to resurrection and immortality. But during the

Middle Kingdom (*ca.* 2050-1650 B.C.) some of the nobles began to inscribe these formulae on the sides of their coffins; and during the New Kingdom (1552-1080 B.C.) certain of the texts were incorporated into the popular Book of the Dead, written mainly on rolls of papyrus.

Originating as they did over a period of centuries, the Pyramid Texts obviously do not represent any unified, consistent system of theology. The great majority of them give precedence to the sun-god, Re, but many are also directed to Osiris, the god of the underworld, who represented death and resurrection.

The Pyramid Texts were evidently meant to be recited, often by a priest, sometimes by the dead king himself. Thus each utterance begins with a conventional rhetorical expression, here rendered as "To say." In the tombs themselves, the particular Pharaoh for whom the text was intended is indicated by a letter abbreviation, e.g., "P" for Pepi I, "M" for Merenre, etc. In this translation the letter "N" (*nomen*) is employed throughout for all Pharaohs' names.

The brief selections from the Pyramid Texts which follow indicate the immense importance attached to the Pharaoh's life after death and demonstrate something of the complications of Egyptian theology.

FROM THE PYRAMID TEXTS

Utterance 570/New-Birth of the Deceased King as a God in Heaven

To say: The face of heaven is washed; the vault of heaven is
    bright;[1]
a god is brought to birth by the sky upon the arms of Shu and
    Tefnut, upon the arms of N.[2]
"Great [sun],"[3] say the gods;
"hear it, this word which N. says to thee;

From *The Pyramid Texts*, Samuel A. B. Mercer, ed. and trans., London: Longmans, Green and Company, 1952. Reprinted by permission of David McKay Company, Inc.

1. "The face of heaven" is the face of the goddess Nut, who personifies the sky. "The vault of heaven" probably refers to the appearance of the sky after a rain.

2. Shu was the god of the air or dryness and his consort Tefnut was the goddess of moisture.

3. Here as in other instances the Mercer translation retains the Egyptian

let thy heart be glad for this N., for this N. is a Great One, the
    son of a Great One;

N. is with thee; take this N. for life, joy, and eternity, with
    thee."

"Khepri,[4] hear it, this word, which is spoken to thee by N.;

let thy heart be glad for N., for N. is a Great One, the son of
    a Great One;

N. is with thee; take him with thee."

"Nun,[5] hear it, this word, which is spoken to thee by N.;

let thy heart be glad for N., for N. is a Great One, the son of
    a Great One;

N. is with thee; take him with thee."

"Atum,[6] hear it, this word, which is spoken to thee by N.;

let thy heart be glad for N., for N. is a Great One, the son of
    a Great One;

N. is with thee; take him with thee."

"[The honored one], son of Geb; [the mighty one], son of Osiris,[7]
    hear it, this word is spoken to thee by N.;

let thy heart be glad for N., for N. is a Great One, the son of
    a Great One;

N. is with thee; take him with thee."

Mayest thou be near to N., in thy name of "Re"[8]; drive thou
    away the garments (darkness) of the sky.

---

syllables, thus: " 'Great *wbn*,' say the gods," etc., *wbn* probably being an
epithet for the personified and deified sun. For the sake of easier read-
ability, we have in such cases omitted the Egyptian word and supplied the
closest available English equivalent in brackets.

4. The form of the sun-god as it appeared in the morning.

5. The all-encircling ocean, the primeval abyss out of which all things
arose, personified as a god.

6. Originally a creator god, Atum appears here as the form of the sun-
god in the evening.

7. Geb was the earth-god and speaker for the gods. Osiris was the judge of
the dead, father of Horus and of the dead king. According to Egyptian
legend, Osiris was murdered by his brother, the god Set. Like nature itself,
he died to rise again. He became the dying, but resurrected and immortal god,
who shared with his followers his kingdom in the underworld.

8. Re was the sun-god and chief of all the gods, appearing also as Khepri
in the morning, Re in the middle of the day, and Atum in the evening. He
was thought to pass through the underworld at night, to rise again in the

May Horus of the Horizon[9] cause him to hear his glory and his
    praise.
out of the mouth of the Two Enneads.[10]
"How beautiful art thou," said his mother; "(mine) heir," said
    Osiris.
N. has not swallowed the eye of Horus,[11]
so that men might say, "he will die for that."
N. has not swallowed a limb of Osiris,
so that the gods might say, "he will die for that."
N. lives on the *isnw* (bread of offering) of his father Atum; pro-
    tect him, [Nut?][12]
thou hast protected N., [Nut], in the princely house which is
    in Heliopolis.
Thou hast commended him to him who is within his *hnti* (two
    limits),[13]
that N. may be expedited.
He who is within his *hnti* (two limits) has recommended N. to
    him who is on his carrying litter,[14]
that N. may be expedited.
N. has escaped his day of death,
even as Set escaped his day of death;[15]
N. has escaped the half-months of death,
even as Set escaped his half-months of death;
N. has escaped his months of death,
even as Set escaped his months of death;

---

morning. The deceased king was often called the son, the faithful follower
and servant of Re.
  9. This is Horus the Elder, distinct from Horus the son of Osiris. In the
Pyramid Texts, this Horus is the living king; Osiris is the dead king, his
predecessor on the throne.
  10. The Great Ennead consisted of the nine gods, Atum, Shu, Tefnut, Geb,
Nut, Osiris, Isis, Set, and Nephthys. A Small Ennead was formed later; we
do not know its exact composition.
  11. The right eye of Horus was the sun and the left eye the moon. The
god Set had committed the sacrilege of swallowing the eye of Horus (or
the sacrificial offering representing the eye).
  12. The goddess personifying the sky.
  13. I.e., birth and death.
  14. This doubtless refers to (the dead) Osiris.
  15. According to legend, an ancient Set-king escaped death through the
mystical rite of hoeing the fields, thus establishing fertility.

N. has escaped the year of death,
even as Set escaped his year of death,
by ploughing the earth. The hands of N. support Nut, like Shu,
even the bones of N. which are firm (or, iron; or, copper), and
    his imperishable limbs;
for N. is a star, the light-scatterer of the sky.[16]
Let N. ascend to the god; let N. be avenged,
so that heaven may not be void of N., so that earth (lit.: this
    land, i.e., Egypt) may not be void of N., for ever.[17]
N. lives a life in accordance with your rule,
O gods of the lower sky, imperishable stars,[18]
which traverse the land of Libya, which are supported by their
    d'm-sceptres;
just as N. is supported, with you, by a *wzs*-sceptre and a *d'm*-
    sceptre.[19]
N. is your fourth,[20]
O gods of the lower sky, imperishable stars,
which traverse the land of Libya, which are supported by their
    d'm-sceptres;
just as N. is supported, with you, by a *wzs*-sceptre and a *d'm*-
    sceptre.
N. is your fourth,
O gods of the lower sky, imperishable stars,
which traverse the land of Libya, which are supported by their
    d'm-sceptres;
just as N. is supported, with you, by a *wzs*-sceptre and a *d'm*-
    sceptre,
by command of Horus, hereditary prince and king of the gods.[21]

16. I.e., Pharaoh, like a star, is imperishable.
17. The deceased king may be immortal both in heaven as one of the
blessed dead and on earth as a perpetual presence.
18. The "lower sky" is the opposite and double of the sky above. The stars
were thought to travel through Libya on their way to the lower sky.
19. The *d'm*-sceptre was connected with law and order; the *wzs*-sceptre was
a symbol of royalty.
20. Four was a sacred number in ancient Egypt. In this case, the "gods of
the lower sky" were counted as one; the imperishable stars, two; the gods
of Libya, three; and the deceased king, four.
21. The title "hereditary prince of the gods" was generally applied to Geb.
In later times, Amun-Re of Thebes was considered "king of the gods."

N. seizes the white crown; that upon which is the wire of the green crown.[22]

N. is the [springing] serpent, which comes forth from Set, which was robbed, but which was returned.[23]

N. was robbed; he is returned; he is made alive.

N. is this (kind of) colour which comes out of Nun.

N. is the eye of Horus, which was not chewed, nor spit out;

he is not chewed nor spit out.

Hear it, this word, O Re, said by N. to thee;

"Thy body is in N., O Re, let thy body live in N., O Re."[24]

"The baboon is a wild-ox," so said [the evil bird];[25]

"[The evil bird] is a wild-ox," so said the baboon.

O that castrated one! O this man! O he who hurries him who hurries (?), among you two![25]

These—this first corporation of the company of the justified

was born before there was any anger;[26]

was born before there was any clamour (lit.: voice);

was born before there was any strife;

was born before there was any conflict;

was born before the eye of Horus was plucked out; before the testicles of Set were torn away.

N. is blood which came from Isis; N. is red blood which came from Nephthys.[27]

N. does *dh'wz* against his *bnw*;[28] there is nothing which the gods can do against N.;

22. The green crown was that of Lower Egypt. The white crown was the emblem of Upper Egypt.

23. The "springing serpent," symbolized as the "eye of Horus on the forehead of Set," was robbed by the South from the North, but later returned following the conquest of the North by Menes. Thus the "eye of Horus" in Heliopolis was the healed one, returned from the South.

24. I.e., the dead king desires to be absorbed into, or identified with, the sun-god.

25. The bird and the baboon pay each other false compliments. Animals are used here to represent men, i.e., flattery as an example of the decline of morals, whereby a castrated bull may be regarded with admiration!

26. The "corporation of the justified" evidently refers to the mass of righteous people in the old days, the pre-historic age before the fight between Horus and Set for the sovereignty.

27. I.e., the king is represented as the son of both Isis and Nephthys.

28. The meaning of these words is unknown, except that *bnw* evidently denotes a part of the body.

N. is the deputy of Re; N. shall not die.
Hear, O Geb, hereditary prince of all the gods, endue him with
his form.[29]
Hear, O Thot, who are among the peaceful ones of the gods,
let a door for N. be opened by Horus; let N. be protected by
Set.[30]
N. appears in the eastern side of the sky,
like Re who shines in the eastern side of the sky.

29. Refers either to the form of Osiris, or to the king's own proper form as
an immortal.
30. This request seems to reflect a period when Horus and Set were at
peace, perhaps during the Second Dynasty.

Utterance 577/The Resurrection of Osiris
with Whom the Gods Are Satisfied

This utterance is an Osirian text of litany-like, poetic structure. The
"king in Osiris" is treated as a dual personality, now as the god
Osiris, now as the deceased king. In this text, the dead king is
resurrected as Osiris; he is welcomed to heaven by the other gods;
the relationship of the king to Osiris is explained; and the king visits
heaven, but returns.

In being absorbed into Osiris, the dead Pharaoh does not lose his
identity. As in the case of Atum-Re, where both Atum and Re are
sun-gods but nonetheless distinct personalities, so Pharaoh and Osiris
are united but separate at the same time. This identification of di-
vinities, while contradictory from a logical standpoint, has many
analogies in the history of religions.

To say: Osiris dawns, pure, mighty; high, lord of truth
on the first of the year; lord of the year.[1]
Atum father of the gods is satisfied; Shu and Tefnut are satisfied; Geb and Nut are satisfied;[2]

1. The resurrection of Osiris was regarded as the cause of the Nile's annual
inundation, which marked the beginning of the Egyptian year.
2. Shu and Tefnut were the children of Atum (or Re); Geb and Nut the
children of Shu and Tefnut.

Osiris and [Isis] are satisfied; Set and [Neit] (Nephthys?) are
satisfied;[3]
all the gods who are in heaven are satisfied; all the gods who
are on earth and in the lands are satisfied;
all the southern and northern gods are satisfied; all the western
and eastern gods are satisfied;
all the nome gods are satisfied; all the city gods are satisfied
with the great and mighty word, which comes forth from the
mouth of Thot, concerning Osiris,[4]
the seal of life, the seal of the gods.
Anubis, the counter of hearts, deducts Osiris N. from the gods
who belong to the earth, (and assigns him) to the gods who
are in heaven,[5]
lord of wine at the inundation.[6]
His year is calculated for him; his hour knows him.[7]
N. is known by his year which is with him;
his hour which is with him knows him.
"Come, my child," says Atum, "come to us," say they, say the
gods to thee, Osiris.
("Our") brother is come to us, the eldest, the first (begotten) of
his father, the first (born) of his mother,"[8]
say they, say the gods.
Heaven conceived him: [the twilight] gave him birth;[9]
N. was conceived with him by heaven;
N. was given birth with him by [the twilight].
Thou supported the sky on thy right side, having life;[10]

3. These were the four children of Geb and Nut, who together with their
five ancestors comprised the so-called Ennead ("Nine").
4. Thot was the herald who announced the decision of the gods in regard
to Osiris as king.
5. Anubis was the ancient mortuary god. Assigning an Osirian king to
heaven appears anomalous, since Osiris is the god of the underworld.
6. Osiris was the lord of the wine-cellar at a great feast which was probably connected with the flooding of the Nile.
7. Osiris's time was calculated according to the inundation of the Nile.
8. Geb was the father and Nut the mother of Osiris. Osiris and the king
were one in conception and birth, two-in-one and one-in-two.
9. This may refer to the evening twilight when a star is born, and the
morning twilight when a deity is born.
10. This refers to the legend of the death of Osiris and the finding of his
body lying on its left side, supporting the sky on its right side.

thou livest, because the gods ordained that thou live.[11]

N. supports the sky on his right side, having life;

he lives his life, because the gods have ordained that he live.

Thou leanest on the earth on thy left side, having joy;

thou livest thy life, because the gods have ordained that thou
    live.

N. leans on the [earth] on his left side, having life (or joy?);

he lives his life, because (the gods) have ordained that he live.

N. ascended on the eastern side of the sky;[12]

he descends as a green bird;

he descends . . . lord of the [twilight] lakes.[13]

N. is purified in the lakes of the *smn*-goose.[14]

11. Osiris failed to die because the gods commanded that he live.
12. The eastern side of the sky was particularly sacred to the early Egyptians. Here the king ascended to heaven.
13. The king descends from the sky where he has been as a star. The "twilight lakes" were originally placed in the sky, where the deceased king would join the imperishable, circumpolar stars which know no destruction, and where he would therefore live forever. Later this twilight region was transferred to the underworld, developing into the realm of Osiris.
14. The *smn*-goose was in later times connected with Amun.

Introduction to *The Admonitions of an Egyptian Sage*

The "Admonitions" belongs to a type of composition popular in Egypt because of the eloquence and wisdom of the discourse, with the actual narrative providing merely a framework. From a historical standpoint, however, it is the account of contemporary events which interests us most.

The "sage" of this work is one Ipuwer, of whom history records nothing except his name. Whether he was a prophet in the Hebrew sense, or merely an observer of events, we do not know, though the latter conjecture appears more likely. He is here represented as holding an impassioned discourse before the Pharaoh and his court. Describing the evils which have overtaken Egypt—civil war, foreign invasion, and social upheaval—he exhorts the king, living peacefully in his palace surrounded by courtiers who conceal the truth from him, to take energetic measures to remedy the situation. The Pharaoh in question may be the aged Phiops II, last monarch of the Sixth Dynasty, who according to tradition came to the throne at age six and reigned for ninety-three years. This reign, which brought to an end the "Old Kingdom" (around 2170 B.C.), ushered in an era of civil strife and disorder. For the next 250 years, historical records of Egypt virtually cease; and those few which remain show that civilization had declined.

Only one manuscript of the "Admonitions" is extant, and this in a very inferior condition. The beginning and the end of the text are missing, and the body of the work is replete with errors and omissions. The spelling and language indicate that the manuscript dates from the Middle Kingdom, though the period described is obviously much earlier. The scribe was apparently copying from an earlier papyrus which in many cases he could not decipher. Thus the translation and interpretation of the composition are in many instances very tentative, and in places impossible.

The text reproduced here covers about the first two-thirds of the translation—Ipuwer's account of the events of his time. The remainder consists mainly of "admonitions": denunciations and exhortations to Pharaoh to "remember" various (traditional) ceremonies and religious observances, after which the text reverts to the description of bloodshed and anarchy.

THE ADMONITIONS OF AN EGYPTIAN SAGE

. . . The door[-keepers] say: Let us go and plunder. The confectioners. . . . The washerman refuses (?) to carry his load. . . . The bird [-catchers] have drawn up in line of battle. . . . [The inhabitants?] of the Marshes carry shields:[1] The brewers . . . sad. A man looks upon his son as his enemy; . . . .

. . . to (?) another. Come . . . predestined for you in the time of Horus, in the age of [the Ennead][2]. . . . The virtuous man walks in mourning (?) on account of that which has hap-

From *The Admonitions of an Egyptian Sage*, Alan H. Gardiner, ed. and trans., Leipzig: J. C. Hinrich, 1909, pp. 19-69.

1. The evils of war are everywhere evident; men abandon their trades to become soldiers.

2. The present disasters were decreed by fate in the age when the gods reigned on earth.

pened in the land. The . . . walks. . . . The tribes of the desert (?) have become Egyptians³ (?) everywhere.

Forsooth, the face is pale (?) . . . which (?) the ancestors had foretold. . . .

[Forsooth] . . . the land full of confederates.⁴ A man goes out to plough with his shield.

Forsooth, the meek say . . . [The man who is . . . of] face is like him who. . . .

Forsooth, the face is pale (?). The bowman is ready. The wrongdoer is everywhere. There is no man of yesterday.⁵

Forsooth, the plunderer (?) . . . everywhere. The servant . . . to find it.

Forsooth, Nile overflows, (yet) no one ploughs for him.⁶ Every man says: we know not what has happened throughout the land.

Forsooth, women are lacking, and no (children) are conceived. Khnum⁷ fashions (mankind) no longer because of the condition of the land.

Forsooth, poor men are become owners of good things. He who could make for himself no sandals is (now) the possessor of riches.

Forsooth, men's slaves, their hearts are sad. Princes do not fraternize with their people (?), when they rejoice (?).

Forsooth, (men's) hearts are violent. Plague is throughout the land. Blood is everywhere. Death is not lacking (?). The mummycloth (?) speaks, before ever one comes near it (?).⁸

Forsooth, many dead men are buried in the river. The stream is a sepulchre, and the place of embalmment has become stream.⁹

3. Literally, real "men" (in distinction to barbarians). Foreigners have become so entrenched in the land that they are regarded as Egyptians.

4. I.e., the confederates of wrongdoers.

5. The meaning probably is: times are so changed that the (virtuous) men of former days have disappeared; only upstarts are in evidence.

6. The Nile personified as a god. No one has enough confidence in the future to till the fields.

7. The god who fashions all mankind.

8. The sense appears to be: corpses are everywhere. Even the mummy-cloths cry out, so that they can be heard at a distance.

9. I.e., the corpses are too numerous to be buried, thus are deposited in the river.

Forsooth, the wealthy are in mourning. The poor man is full of joy. Every town says: let us suppress the powerful among us.

Forsooth, men are like *gm*-birds.[10] Squalor (?) is throughout the land. There is none whose clothes are white in these times.

Forsooth, the land turns round as does a potter's wheel. The robber is a possessor of riches. (The rich man?) is [become?] a plunderer.[11]

Forsooth, trusty servants (?) are [like]. . . . The poor man [complains?]: how terrible it is (?), what am I to do?

Forsooth, the river is blood, and (yet) men drink of it. Men shrink from (?) (tasting?) human beings, and thirst after water.

Forsooth, gates, columns and walls (?) are consumed by fire; (while) the . . . of the king's palace stands firm and endures.

Forsooth, the ship of the [Southerners][12] has gone adrift (?). The towns are destroyed. Upper Egypt has become dry [wastes?].

Forsooth, crocodiles are glutted (?) with what they have captured. Men go to them of their own accord. It fares ill with the earth too (??). People say: walk not here, behold it is a . . . Behold people tread [upon the earth?] like fishes. The timid man does not (?) distinguish it through terror.[13]

Forsooth, men are few. He who places his brother in the ground is everywhere (?).[14] When the officiants (?)[15] have spoken (?), he [flees?] without delay.

Forsooth, the well-born man . . . without being recognized (?). The child of his lady has become the son of his maid-servant.[16]

10. Similar to a heron: the allusion may be either to its grayish coloring or to its habit of wallowing in the mud.
11. I.e., the world is turned upside down: he who was a robber is now rich, while the one-time rich man has become a robber.
12. Probably a metaphorical expression for the "ship of state" of Upper Egypt.
13. Perhaps the meaning is: the crocodiles have more than enough to feed upon; men commit suicide by throwing themselves into the river as their prey. On land, people warn each other to avoid certain places. In their terror, men can no longer distinguish the water from the earth.
14. I.e., grave-diggers are everywhere.
15. Perhaps the officiants at a funeral ceremony.
16. Distinctions are no longer made between the child of the head wife and the child of the slave-girl.

Forsooth, the Desert is throughout the Land. The nomes are laid waste. A foreign tribe from abroad has come to Egypt.

Forsooth, people come (?). . . . There are no Egyptians anywhere.

Forsooth, gold and lapis lazuli, silver and malachite, carnelian and bronze, stone of Yebhet and . . . are fastened on the necks of female slaves. Good things are in the land. (Yet) the mistresses of houses say: would that we had something to eat.

Forsooth, . . . noble ladies. Their limbs are in sad plight by reason of (their) rags. Their hearts sink (?) in greeting [one another?].

Forsooth, boxes of ebony are broken up. Precious acacia-wood is cleft asunder. . . .

Forsooth, the builders [of Pyramids (?) have become] field-labourers. Those who were in the divine bark are yoked together (?)[17] Men do not sail northwards to [Byblos][18] today. What shall we do for cedars for our mummies, with the produce of which priests are buried, and with the oil of which [chiefs] are embalmed as far as Keftiu.[19] They come no more. Gold is lacking, the . . . of all handicrafts is at an end (?). The . . . of the king's palace is despoiled (?). What a great thing it is that the people of the Oases come with their festival spices (?) . . . with fresh redmet-plants . . . of birds. . . .[20]

Forsooth, Elephantine and Thinis (?) are [the dominion of?] Upper Egypt (?), (yet) without paying taxes owing to civil strife.[21] Lacking are grain (?), charcoal, . . . The products of craftsmen . . . the palace. To what purpose is a treasure-house without its revenues? Glad indeed is the heart of the king, when

17. Probably the former nobles and priests, who are now reduced to the position of field-laborers.
18. The port of Lebanon from which the Egyptians obtained their cedars.
19. Probably Crete, which maintained contacts with Egypt at an early date.
20. I.e., the costly materials indispensable in the rites of embalmment and for the construction of the divine barks in the temples are no longer obtainable in Egypt, although the chieftains of distant Crete still use them. Egyptians must consider themselves fortunate to obtain the comparatively trivial products of the Oases.
21. This may mean that the dominion of Upper Egypt is now restricted to the country between Elephantine and Thinis—the actual limits of the kingdom at one point during the Eleventh Dynasty.

Truth comes to him![22] Lo, every foreign country [comes?]! That is our water! That is our happiness! What shall we do in respect thereof? All is ruin!

Forsooth, mirth has perished, and is [no longer] made. It is groaning that is throughout the land, mingled with lamentations.

Forsooth, all dead are like those who live (??). Those who were Egyptians (?) have become foreigners (?). . . .

Forsooth, hair has fallen out for everyone.[23] The son of a man of rank is no (longer) distinguished from him who has no such father (?).

Forsooth . . . on account of noise. Noise is not lacking (??) in years of noise. There is no end [to] noise.

Forsooth, great and small [say]: I wish I might die. Little children say (?): he ought never to have caused [me] to live (??).

Forsooth, the children of princes are dashed against the walls. The offspring of desire are laid out on the high ground.[24] Khnum groans because of his weariness.[25]

Forsooth, those who were in the place of embalmment are laid on the high ground. It is the secret of the embalmers (?). . . .[26]

Forsooth, the Marshlands in their entirety are not hidden.[27] Lower Egypt can boast of trodden roads. What shall one do? There are no . . . anywhere. People shall surely (?) say: cursed be (?) the secret place! Behold, it is in the hands of (?) those who knew it not like those who knew it. The Asiatics are skilled in the crafts of the Marshlands.

Forsooth let citizens be (?) placed over corn-rubbers (?).[28]

22. This sentence may be meant ironically: in his poverty, the king must consider himself happy if he obtains Truth in lieu of tribute.
23. This may refer to the side-lock worn by the children of the wealthy as a sign of their rank.
24. Perhaps: poverty drives people to kill their children by exposure.
25. Probably the sense is: the god Khnum groans with the exertion of creating children who are doomed to an early death.
26. Perhaps: the secret art of the embalmers is thereby made useless.
27. The natural protection of the Delta marshlands is now rendered useless, since foreigners have entered and made themselves masters of the crafts of those regions.
28. The stones upon which female slaves grind corn. This probably means that citizens are degraded to the lowest menial duties.

Those who were clad in fine linen are beaten . . . (?) Those who never saw the day go forth unhindered (?).[29] Those who were on the couches of their husbands, let them sleep upon . . . of (?). . . . I say (?) "it is heavy to me" concerning (?) . . . laden with *ntiw*-oil. Load them (?) with vessels filled with . . . [Let?] them know the palanquin.[30] As for the butler, wear him out (??). Good are the remedies thereof! Noble ladies suffer (?) like slave-girls. Musicians are in (?) the chambers within the halls (?). What they sing to the goddess Mert[31] (?) is dirges (?). Story-tellers (?) . . . over the corn-rubbers.

Forsooth, all female slaves are free with their tongues. When their mistress speaks, it is irksome to the servants.

Forsooth, trees are destroyed (?). . . . I have separated him and the slaves of his house. People will say, when they hear of it: destroyed are cakes (?) for most (?) children. There is no food. . . . Today, like what is the taste[32] thereof today?

Forsooth, princes are hungry and in distress. Servants are served (?) . . . by reason of mourning.

Forsooth, the hot-headed (?) man says: If I knew where God is, then would I make offerings unto him.

Forsooth, [Right?] is throughout the land in this its name. What men do, in appealing to it, is Wrong.

Forsooth, runners . . . robber. All his property is carried off.

Forsooth, all animals, their hearts weep. Cattle moan because of the state of the land.

(Several very fragmentary passages follow.)

Forsooth, the ways are. . . . The roads are guarded.[33] Men sit over the bushes until the benighted (traveller) comes, in order to plunder his burden. What is upon him is taken away. He is belaboured with blows of the stick, and slain wrongfully.

Forsooth, that has perished, which yesterday was seen (?).

29. Probably: ladies of high rank who used to live in houses must now toil outdoors in the heat.
30. I.e., if something laden with *ntiw*-oil is heavy, then let them know the weight of the palanquin! Do not spare your servants!
31. A patron of music.
32. "Taste" is used metaphorically for the taste of evil and death.
33. By robbers?

The land is left over to its weariness (?) like the cutting of
flax.[34] Poor men . . . are in affliction. . . . Would that there
might be an end of men, no conception, no birth! O that the
earth would cease from noise, and tumult be no more!

Forsooth, [men eat] herbs, and wash (them) down with
water. No fruit (?) nor herbs are found [for] the birds. . . . is
taken away from the mouth of the swine . . . hunger.[35]

Forsooth, grain has perished on every side. (People) are
stripped of clothes, spices (?) and oil. Everybody says: there is
none. The storehouse is ruined. Its keeper is stretched on the
ground. It is no (?) happy thing for my heart (??). . . .
Would that I had made my voice (heard) at that moment, that
it might save me from the pain in which I am (?).

Forsooth, the splendid (?) judgement-hall, its writings are
taken away. Laid bare is the secret place that was (such formerly??).

Forsooth, magical spells are divulged. Sm-incantations (?)
and shn-incantations (?) are frustrated (?) because they are
remembered by men.[36]

Forsooth, public offices are opened and [their] census-lists
are taken away.[37] Serfs become lords of serfs (?).

Forsooth . . . [officials] are slain, and their writings are
taken away. Woe is me because of the misery in this time!

Forsooth, the scribes of the tm} (m),[38] their writings are destroyed. The corn (?) of Egypt is common property.[39]

Forsooth, the laws of the judgement-hall are cast forth. Men
walk upon [them] in the public places. Poor men break them
up (?) in the streets.

34. The land is as desolate as a mown field. No stubble is ever left in the
flax-fields.
35. Men are reduced to eating the food of animals, so that nothing is left
over for the animals.
36. Magic must be mysterious to be effective; by becoming known, magical
spells are profaned.
37. Destruction of the census-lists would eliminate the records of slavery,
permitting slaves to claim an independence to which they were not legally
entitled.
38. This word has some reference to agriculture.
39. I.e., the documents regarding the distribution of corn were lost.

Forsooth, the poor man has come to the estate (?) of the divine Ennead.[40] That (former) procedure of the houses of the Thirty is divulged.[41]

Forsooth, the great judgement-hall is thronged (?). Poor men come and go in the Great Houses.[42]

Forsooth, the children of princes are cast out (?) in the streets. He who knows says it is so. He who is ignorant says no. He who does not know it, it is good in his eyes (?).[43]

Behold, the fire has mounted up on high. Its burning goes forth against the enemies of the land.[44]

Behold, things are done, that have never happened for long time past (?): the king has been taken away (?) by poor men.[45]

Behold, he who was buried as a hawk is[46] . . . What the pyramid concealed is become empty.[47]

Behold, a few lawless men have ventured to despoil the land of the kingship.

Behold, men have ventured to rebel against the Uraeus,[48] the . . . of Re, which pacifies the two lands.

Behold, the secret of the land, whose limits were unknown, is divulged.[49] The Residence is overturned in a minute.

Behold, Egypt has come to pour out water.[50] He who poured water on the ground, he has captured the strong man in misery (??).

40. The meaning is perhaps that through the publicity now given to the legal code, poor men presume to sit in judgment like the gods of the Ennead.
41. Probably a court of thirty judges existed in Egypt at some early period.
42. The six Great Houses were the ancient high courts of Egypt. Now the rabble has taken them over.
43. Perhaps: to the ignorant man, things seem quite in order. Might this unsuspecting person be the king?
44. The "fire" referred to must be an image for the accumulated evils previously described, a fire so terrible that it is now about to consume even the enemies of the land.
45. Possibly a reference to the robbery of royal tombs.
46. The king was commonly compared to a hawk flying to heaven.
47. The sarcophagus?
48. The serpent-diadem of the king and of the sun-god.
49. Perhaps: secret affairs of which formerly only the king had full knowledge.
50. As an offering; this may have been regarded as a servile action.

Behold, the Serpent is taken from its hole.[51] The secrets of the kings of Upper and Lower Egypt are divulged.

Behold, the Residence is afraid through want. . . . in order to (?) stir feuds unopposed.

Behold, the land has . . . with confederates. The brave man, the coward takes away his property.

Behold, the Serpent . . . the dead. He who could make for himself no sarcophagus is (now) possessor of a tomb.

Behold, the possessors of tombs are driven out on the high ground. He who could make for himself no coffin is (now) [possessor] of a treasury (?).

Behold, this has happened [to?] men: he who could not build himself a cell is now possessor of walls.

Behold, the judges of the land are driven out through the land. The . . . are driven out from the houses of kings.

Behold, noble ladies are upon . . . Princes are in the storehouse.[52] He who never slept upon walls[53] (?) is (now) the possessor of a bed.

Behold, the possessor of wealth (now) passes the night thirsting. He who begged for himself his dregs is (now) the possessor of bowls full to overflowing (?).

Behold, the possessors of robes are (now) in rags. He who never wove for himself is (now) the possessor of fine linen.

Behold, he who never built for himself a boat is (now) possessor of ships. He who possessed the same looks at them, but they are not his.

Behold, he who had no shade is (now) the possessor of shade. The possessors of shade are . . . storm.[54]

51. The spirit of a place or a family, conceived in the form of a serpent. Here the spirit of the old Pharaonic stock must be meant.

52. The "storehouse" is often mentioned in Egyptian texts as the place where the slaves taken in war were confined or employed. To say that "princes are in the storehouse" is equivalent to saying that they are reduced to the position of slaves.

53. Perhaps meaning: he who never slept *even* upon a wall, where he would be safer from snakes and scorpions than if he slept upon the ground.

54. The first clause must mean: he who was formerly unable to shelter himself from the sun can now do so. The second clause must somehow contain an antithesis to the first, such as: "those who (formerly) found shelter are now exposed to the stormy winds."

Behold, he who was ignorant of the lyre (now) possesses a harp. He who never sang for himself (now) vaunts the goddess Mert.[55]

Behold, those who possessed vessel-stands of bronze—not one jug is adorned for one of them (??).[56]

Behold, he who slept without a wife (?) through want finds precious things. He whom he never saw (?) stands and . . . (?).

Behold, he who possessed no property is (now) a man of wealth. The prince praises him.[57]

Behold, the poor of the land have become rich, and [the possessor of] property has become one who has nothing.

Behold, . . . have become masters of butlers. He who was a messenger (now) sends another.

Behold, he who had no loaf is owner of a barn. His magazine is provided with the possessions of another.

Behold, he whose hair had fallen out and who was without oil is become a possessor of jars of sweet myrrh.

Behold, she who had no box is possessor of a coffer. She who looked at her face in the water is possessor of a mirror.

Behold, ...

Behold, a man is happy when he eats his food. "Partake of thy possessions in joy of heart, turning not back! It is good for a man to eat his food." The god allows it to him whom he praises. . . . [Behold, he who was ignorant of] his god (now) offers to him with the incense of another; not known. . . .

Behold, noble ladies, great ladies, mistresses of goodly things give their children for beds (?).[58]

Behold, a man [who . . . obtains] a noble lady as wife; her father protects him. He who has not . . . slay him.[59]

Behold, the children of courtiers are [in rags?]. . . . [Rich men hand over the] calves (??) of their cows (?) to plunderers.

55. The patron of music.
56. This perhaps refers to the custom of wreathing wine-jars with garlands.
57. I.e., princes now have to adopt an attitude of deference toward men who were formerly poverty-stricken.
58. In exchange for beds?
59. Probably: the man with no one to protect him is killed.

Behold, butchers transgress (?) with the cattle of the poor . . . plunderers.[60]

Behold, he who never slaughtered for himself now slaughters bulls. He who knew not . . . sees . . . all. . . .

Behold, butchers transgress (?) with geese. They are given [to] the gods instead of oxen.[61]

Behold, female slaves . . . offer geese (?). Noble ladies. . . .

Behold, noble ladies flee. The overseers (?). . . . Their [children?] are cast down through fear of death.

[Behold] the chiefs of the land flee. There is no . . . for them because of want. . . .

[Behold], those who possessed beds (now lie) on the ground. He who passed the night in squalor (?) is (now) one who prepares (?) for himself a waterskin (?).

Behold noble ladies go hungry; the butchers are sated with what was prepared for them.[62]

Behold, no offices are in their (right) place, like a frightened herd without a herdsman.

Behold, cattle are left to stray, and there is none to gather them together. Each man fetches for himself those that are branded with his name.

Behold, a man is slain beside his brother. He . . . to save his (own) limbs.[63]

Behold, he who had no yoke of oxen is (now) possessor of a herd. He who could find for himself no oxen to plough with is (now) possessor of cattle.

Behold, he who had no grain is (now) the possessor of granaries. He who had to fetch for himself *tȝbt*-corn (now) sends it forth.

Behold, he who had no dependents (?) is now a lord of serfs. He who was a [notable] does commission(s) himself.

Behold, the powerful men of the land, the condition of the people is not reported (to them??). All is ruin!

60. I.e., slay indiscriminately.
61. Perhaps: the new rich give geese as offerings and eat the oxen themselves.
62. Perhaps: that which was formerly prepared for the ladies who are now famished.
63. Perhaps: a man abandons his brother to save himself?

Behold, no craftsmen work. The enemies of the land have spoilt (?) its crafts (?).

[Behold, he who gathered in?] the harvest (now) knows nothing thereof. He who never ploughed [for himself] . . . [The reaping?] takes place, but is not reported. The scribe [sits in his office (?), but] his hands are [idle?] within it.⁶⁴

64. This refers to the decay of agriculture and to the laxity of government officials in collecting the tax on corn.

Introduction to *The Story of Si-nuhe*

The Si-nuhe of this tale was an Egyptian official of some importance serving the daughter of Amen-em-het I—in what capacity he does not say. When that king died (*ca.* 1962 B.C.), Si-nuhe suddenly fled into exile in Syria. We can only guess at the reasons for this move: Si-nuhe himself takes care to conceal them. Perhaps he feared the prospect of civil war between rival contenders to the throne (other sources indicate the existence of a palace conspiracy at about this time); and certainly the period of transition between kings was a dangerous one for an official not fully identified with the new ruler. No doubt Si-nuhe had other reasons as well, though later both he and the new Pharaoh, Sen-Usert I, make a point of protesting his innocence of all wrongdoing.

Si-nuhe may have been a real historical personage, though no mention of him other than the following story has survived the centuries. But even if fictional, his character and the account of his life ring true, corresponding to what we know of Syria-Palestine in that period from Old Testament and other sources. It has been pointed out that the story of Si-nuhe resembles the autobiographies commonly inscribed upon the walls of tombs: perhaps such an inscription furnished the nucleus from which the literary work was later elaborated.

The tale is full of elaborate poetic expressions which strike the modern reader as artificial, though perhaps to the ancient Egyptian they added to the story's appeal. No doubt the sentiment of love of country also struck a responsive chord in those Egyptians of a later day serving far from home in the territories of a far-flung empire. In any event, the popularity of the work is attested by the extraordinary number of copies and quotations from it which have come down to us. Undoubtedly the story of Si-nuhe was one of the classics of ancient Egyptian literature.

THE STORY OF SI-NUHE

THE HEREDITARY PRINCE AND COUNT, Judge and District Overseer of the domains of the Sovereign in the lands of the Asiatics, real acquaintance of the king, his beloved, the Attendant Si-nuhe. He says:

I was an attendant who followed his lord, a servant of the royal harem (and of) the Hereditary Princess, the great of favor, the wife of King Sen-Usert[1] in (the pyramid town) Khenem-sut, the daughter of King Amen-em-het[2] in (the pyramid town) Qa-nefru, Nefru, the lady of reverence.

YEAR 30, THIRD MONTH OF THE FIRST SEASON, DAY 7.[3] The god ascended to his horizon,[4] the King of Upper and Lower Egypt: Sehetep-ib-Re[5] was taken up to heaven and united with the sun disc. The body of the god merged with him who made him.[6] The Residence City was in silence, hearts were in mourning, the Great Double Doors[7] were sealed shut. The courtiers (sat) head on lap, and the people were in grief.

Now his majesty had sent an army to the land of the Temeh[8]-

From *Ancient Near Eastern Texts Relating to the Old Testament*, J. B. Pritchard, ed., John A. Wilson, trans. 2nd ed., Princeton: Princeton University Press, 1950, 1955, pp. 18-22. Copyright 1950, 1955 by Princeton University Press. Reprinted by permission.

1. Sen-Usert (or Sesòstris) I, reigned 1971-1928 B.C. (for nine years reigned jointly with his father, Amen-em-het).
2. Amen-em-het I, reigned 1991-1962 B.C.
3. *Ca.* 1962 B.C., the date of Amen-em-het's death.
4. The dwelling of the sun-god in the sky. Since the Pharaoh was identified with the sun-god, his tomb is also called his "horizon."
5. The official name of Amen-em-het I.
6. At death the Pharaoh was taken back into the body of his father, the sun-god.
7. The entrance to Pharaoh's palace.
8. The Temeh and Tehenu were Libyan tribes who frequently raided the Delta region.

Libyans, with his eldest son as the commander thereof, the good god Sen-Usert, and even now he was returning and had carried off living captives of the Tehenu[8]-Libyans and all (kinds of) cattle without number.

The courtiers of the palace sent to the western border to let the King's Son know the events which had taken place at the court. The messengers met him on the road, and they reached him in the evening time. He did not delay a moment; the falcon[9] flew away with his attendants, without letting his army know it. Now the royal children who had been following him in this army had been sent for, and one of them was summoned.[10] While I was standing (near by) I heard his voice as he was speaking and I was a little way off. My heart was distraught, my arms spread out (in dismay), trembling fell upon all my limbs.[11] I removed myself *by leaps and bounds* to seek a hiding place for myself. I placed myself between two bushes, in order to *cut (myself) off from* the road and its *travel*.

I set out southward, (but) I did not plan to reach this Residence City, (for) I thought that there would be civil disorder, and I did not expect to live after him. I crossed Lake Ma'aty[12] near Sycamore,[12] and I came to Snefru Island.[12] I spent the day there on the *edge* of the fields. I *came into the open* light, while it was *(still)* day, and I met a man standing near by. He stood in awe of me, for he was afraid. When the time of the evening meal came, I drew near to Ox-town.[12] I crossed over in a barge without a rudder,[13] by aid of the west wind. I passed by the east of the quarry above Mistress-of-the-Red-Mountain.[14] I gave (free) road to my feet going northward, and I came up to the Wall-of-the-Ruler,[15] made to oppose the Asiatics and to crush

9. The new king, Sen-Usert I.
10. This seems to refer to a plot to set up a rival king.
11. Note the relation of Si-nuhe's fright to the conversation of the summoned prince.
12. Localities unknown. Apparently Si-nuhe avoided the cultivated stretches of the Delta and crossed the Nile where it is a single stream, somewhere near the location of modern Cairo.
13. A broad vessel such as was employed in the transport of stone.
14. An elevation east of modern Cairo, a source for a kind of reddish-brown sandstone used in statues. The "mistress" is the goddess worshipped there.
15. A fortress on the eastern frontier along the general line of the present Suez Canal, meant to repel the Syrian nomads.

the Sand-Crossers. I took a crouching position in a bush, for fear lest the watchmen upon the wall where their day's (duty) was might see me.

I set out at evening time, and when day broke I reached Peten. I halted at the Island of Kem-wer.[16] An attack of thirst overtook me. I was parched, and my throat was dusty. I said: "This is the taste of death!" (But then) I lifted up my heart and collected myself, for I had heard the sound of the lowing of cattle, and I spied Asiatics. The sheikh among them, who had been in Egypt, recognized me.[17] Then he gave me water while he boiled milk for me. I went with him to his tribe. What they did (for me) was good.[18]

One foreign country gave me to another. I set off for Byblos[19] and approached Qedem,[20] and spent a year and a half there. Ammi-enshi[21]—he was a ruler of Upper Retenu[22]—took me and said to me: "Thou wilt do well with me, and thou wilt hear the speech of Egypt." He said this, for he knew my character, he had heard of my wisdom, and the people of Egypt who were there with him had borne witness for me.

Then he said to me: "Why hast thou come hither? Has something happened in the Residence City?" Then I said to him: "The King of Upper and Lower Egypt: Sehetep-ib-Re is departed to the horizon, and no one knows what might happen because of it." But I said equivocally: "I had come from an expedition to the land of Temeh, when report was made to me. My heart quailed; it carried me off on the way of *flight.* (Yet) no one had gossiped about me; no one had spat in my face; not a belittling word had been heard, nor had my name been heard in the mouth of the herald.[23] I do not know what brought me to this country. It was as though it might be a god."[24]

16. Lakes on the Isthmus of Suez.
17. This indicates that Si-nuhe was well known in Egypt.
18. I.e., they treated me kindly.
19. The port of Lebanon from which the Egyptians imported wood.
20. (Or Kedemi): Semitic word for "the East" in general.
21. An Amorite name unfamiliar to the Egyptian scribe, who tried to egyptianize it to "Amu's son Enshi."
22. The highland country of northern Palestine and south-central Syria.
23. I.e., "There was no official charge against me."
24. I.e., a supernatural intervention.

Then he said to me: "Well, what will that land be like without him, that beneficent god, the fear of whom pervaded foreign
countries like (the fear of) Sekhmet[25] in a year of pestilence?"
I spoke to him that I might answer him: "Well, of course, his
son has entered into the palace and has taken the inheritance
of his father. Moreover, he is a god without his peer. There is no
other who surpasses him. He is a master of understanding, effective in plans and beneficent of decrees. Going forth[26] and
coming back are in conformance with his command. He it was
who subdued the foreign countries while his father was in his
palace, and he reported to him that what had been charged to
him had been carried out. . . .[27] How joyful is this land which
he has ruled! He is one who extends its frontiers. He will carry
off the lands of the south, and he will not consider the northern
countries (seriously), (for) he was made to smite the Asiatics
and to crush the Sand-Crossers. Send to him! Let him know thy
name! Do not utter a curse against his majesty. He will not fail
to do good to the country which shall be loyal to him!"

Then he said to me: "Well, really, Egypt is happy that it
knows that he is flourishing. Now thou art here. Thou shalt
stay with me. What I shall do for thee is good."

He set me at the head of his children. He married me to his
eldest daughter. He let me choose for myself of his country, of
the choicest of that which was with him on his frontier with
another country. It was a good land, named Yaa.[28] Figs were
in it, and grapes. It had more wine than water. Plentiful was
its honey, abundant its olives. Every (kind of) fruit was on its
trees. Barley was there, and emmer. There was no limit to any
(kind of) cattle. Moreover, great was that which accrued to
me[29] as a result of the love of me. He made me ruler of a tribe
of the choicest of his country. Bread was made for me as daily

25. A goddess associated with disease.
26. To war.
27. A series of flattering epithets for Pharaoh is omitted here.
28. Yaa: the precise location of this place is not known, though it must
have been in the general area of northern Palestine or southern Syria
(Retenu). It was close enough to some main road so that Si-nuhe could en-
tertain traveling Egyptians.
29. I.e., "the gifts which I received."

fare, wine as daily provision, cooked meat and roast fowl, beside the wild beasts of the desert, for they hunted for me and laid before me, beside the catch of my (own) hounds. Many . . . were made for me, and milk in every (kind of) cooking.

I spent many years, and my children grew up to be strong men, each man as the restrainer of his (own) tribe. The messenger who went north or who went south to the Residence City[30] stopped over with me, (for) I used to make everybody stop over. I gave water to the thirsty. I put him who had strayed (back) on the road. I rescued him who had been robbed. When the Asiatics became so bold as to oppose the rulers of foreign countries,[31] I counseled their movements. This ruler of (Re)-tenu had me spend many years as commander of his army. Every foreign country against which I went forth, when I had made my attack on it, was driven away from its pasturage and its wells. I plundered its cattle, carried off its inhabitants, took away their food, and slew people in it by my strong arm, by my bow, by my movements, and by my successful plans. I found favor in his heart, he loved me, he recognized my valor, and he placed me at the head of his children, when he saw how my arms flourished.

A mighty man of Retenu came, that he might challenge me in my (own) camp. He was a hero without his peer, and he had repelled all of it.[32] He said that he would fight me, he intended to despoil me, and he planned to plunder my cattle, on the advice of his tribe. That prince discussed (it) with me, and I said: "I do not know him. Certainly I am no confederate of his, so that I might move freely in his encampment. Is it the case that I have (ever) opened his *door* or overthrown his fences? (Rather), it is hostility because he sees me carrying out thy commissions. I am really like a stray bull in the midst of another herd, and a bull of (these) cattle attacks him. . . ."[33]

30. Of the Egyptian king.
31. I.e., of other foreign countries. The Egyptian term used here, *Heqaukhasut*, is the probable origin of the term "Hyksos." This may be an early reference to nomadic peoples who would later participate in the invasion of Egypt.
32. I.e., he had already beaten everyone of the land of Retenu.
33. I.e., Si-nuhe is challenged because he is a foreigner.

During the night I sprung my bow and shot my arrows,[34] I gave free play to my dagger, and polished my weapons. When day broke, (Re)tenu was come. It had *whipped up* its tribes and collected the countries of a (good) half of it. It had thought (only) of this fight. Then he[35] came to me as I was waiting, (for) I had placed myself near him. Every heart burned for me; women and men groaned. Every heart was sick for me. They said: "Is there another strong man who could fight against him?" Then *(he took)* his shield, his battle-axe, and his *armful of javelins. Now* after I had let his weapons issue forth, I made his arrows pass by me uselessly, one close to another. He charged me, and I shot him, my arrow sticking in his neck. He cried out and fell on his nose. I felled him with his (own) battle-axe and raised my cry of victory over his back, while every Asiatic roared. I gave praise to Montu,[36] while his adherents were mourning for him. This ruler Ammi-enshi took me into his embrace. Then I carried off his goods and plundered his cattle. What he had planned to do to me I did to him. I took what was in his tent and stripped his encampment. I became great thereby, I became extensive in my wealth, I became abundant in my cattle.

Thus did god[37] to show mercy to him upon whom he had *laid blame,* whom he had led astray to another country. (But) today his heart is assuaged.[38] . . .

A poetical statement of homesickness for Egypt follows.

Now when the majesty of the King of Upper and Lower Egypt: Kheper-ka-Re, the justified,[39] was told about this situation in which I was,[40] then his majesty kept sending to me with presentations from the royal presence, that he might gladden

34. Probably for practice.
35. Si-nuhe's opponent.
36. (Month): the Egyptian god of war.
37. The god: probably the king of Egypt, to whose divine power Si-nuhe attributes his success in this combat.
38. Perhaps Si-nuhe atoned for his earlier flight by showing himself to be a successful Egyptian abroad.
39. Sen-Usert I.
40. Perhaps this negotiation was undertaken by one of the envoys whom Si-nuhe was in the habit of entertaining as they passed through his domain.

the heart of this servant[41] like the ruler of any foreign country. The royal children in his palace let me hear their commissions.[42]

COPY OF THE DECREE WHICH WAS BROUGHT TO THIS SERVANT ABOUT BRINGING HIM (BACK) TO EGYPT.

"The Horus: Living in Births; the Two Goddesses: Living in Births; the King of Upper and Lower Egypt: Kheper-ka-Re; the Son of Re: Amen-em-het,[43] living forever and ever. Royal decree to the Attendant Si-nuhe. Behold, this decree of the king is brought to thee to let thee know that:

"Thou hast traversed the foreign countries, starting from Qedem to (Re)tenu. One country gave thee to another, under the advice of thy (own) heart to thee. What hast thou done that anything should be done to thee? Thou hast not cursed, that thy word should be punished. Thou hast not spoken against the counsel of the nobles, that thy speeches should be opposed. This plan (simply) carried away thy heart. It was in no heart against thee. This thy heaven which is in the palace[44] is firm and steadfast today. Her head *is covered* with the kingship of the land.[45] Her children are in the court.

"MAYEST THOU LAY UP TREASURES WHICH THEY MAY GIVE THEE; MAYEST THOU LIVE ON THEIR BOUNTY. Do thou return to Egypt, that thou mayest see the home in which thou didst grow up and kiss the ground at the Great Double Door and join with the courtiers. For today, surely, thou hast begun to grow old; thou hast lost (thy) virility. Recall thou the day of burial, the passing to a revered state,[46] when the evening is set aside for thee with ointments and wrappings from the hand of Tait.[47] A funeral procession is made for thee on the day of interment, a mummy case of gold, with head of lapis lazuli, with the heaven

41. Servant: polite expression for "I."
42. I.e., they also wrote to him.
43. Scribal error for Sen-Usert.
44. The queen.
45. I.e., she wears the insignia of rule.
46. Thy coming to an honored death. The following sentences describe embalming and burial.
47. The goddess of weaving.

above thee,[48] as thou art placed upon a sledge,[49] oxen dragging thee and singers in front of thee, when the dance of the *muu*[50] is performed at the door of thy tomb, when the requirements of the offering table are summoned for thee and there is sacrifice beside thy offering stones, thy pillars[51] being hewn of white stone in the midst of (the tombs of) the royal children. It should not be that thou shouldst die in a foreign country. Asiatics should not escort thee. Thou shouldst not be placed in a sheep-skin when thy wall is made. This is (too) long to be roaming the earth. Give heed to *sickness*, that thou mayest return."[52]

THIS DECREE REACHED ME AS I WAS STANDING IN THE MIDST OF MY TRIBE. It was read to me. I put myself upon my belly; I touched the ground; I scattered it upon my hair. I went about my encampment rejoicing and saying: "How can this be done for a servant whom his heart led astray to barbarous countries? But the indulgence which saved me from death is really good! Thy *ka*[53] will let me effect the end of my body at home!"

COPY OF THE ANSWER TO THIS DECREE. THE SERVANT OF THE PALACE SI-NUHE says:

"In very good peace![54] This flight which this servant made in his ignorance is known by thy *ka*, O good god, Lord of the Two Lands,[55] whom Re loves and whom Montu, Lord of Thebes, favors! . . .[56]

"This is the prayer of this servant to his Lord, the saviour in the West:[57] THE LORD OF PERCEPTION, WHO PERCEIVES PEOPLE,

---

48. The canopy over the hearse, or possibly the lid of the sarcophagus, which was thought to symbolize the sky-goddess, Nut.
49. The common means of transporting heavy loads.
50. A funerary dance.
51. The pillars of the tomb.
52. I.e., you have been following the nomadic life for too long. Remember that you are of an age when a sickness might carry you off and deprive you of burial in Egypt.
53. Usually, the force in a man which keeps him alive, his personality, but here merely a poetic expression for "thou."
54. May you read this writing.
55. Upper and Lower Egypt.
56. This translation omits the good wishes for the king which follow.
57. The realm of the dead.

MAY HE PERCEIVE[58] in the majesty of the palace that this servant
was afraid to say it. It is (still) like something (too) big to repeat.[59] . . . FURTHER, MAY THY MAJESTY COMMAND THAT
THERE BE BROUGHT Maki from Qedem, Khenti-iaush from
Khent-*keshu*, and Menus from the lands of the Fenkhu.[60] They
are *men exact* and reliable, *young men* who grew up in the love
of thee—not to mention (Re)tenu: it is thine, like thy (own)
hounds.[61]

"Now this flight which the servant made, it was not planned,
it was not in my heart, I had not worried about it. I do not
know what severed me from (my) place. It was after the manner of a dream, as if A MAN OF THE DELTA were to see himself
IN ELEPHANTINE,[62] or a man of the (northern) marshes in Nu-
bia.[63] I had not been afraid. No one had run after me. I had not
heard a belittling word. My name had not been heard in the
mouth of the herald. And yet—my body *shuddered*, my feet
were *trembling*, my heart led me on, and the god who ordained
this flight drew me away. I was not at all stiff-backed *formerly*.[64] A man who knows his land should be afraid, (for) Re
has set the fear of thee throughout the earth, and the dread of
thee in every foreign country. Whether I am at home or
whether I am in this place, thou art he who covers this horizon,[65] the sun disc rises at thy pleasure, the water in the River
is drunk as thou wishest, and the air in the sky is breathed as
thou biddest. This servant will hand over THE VIZIERSHIP WHICH
THIS SERVANT HAS EXERCISED IN THIS PLACE."[66]

Then they came for this servant. . . . I was permitted to
spend a day in Yaa handing over my property to my children,

58. I.e., may he perceive Si-nuhe's wish.
59. Si-nuhe feels that his case is too delicate to be stated directly.
60. It is unclear whether Si-nuhe suggests these Asiastics as reliable character witnesses, as hostages, or as escort. Fenkhu: perhaps Phoenicia.
61. I.e., Retenu is well-disposed toward Pharaoh.
62. An island in the first cataract of the Nile: the southern boundary of
Egypt.
63. Region south of Egypt, now northern Sudan.
64. I.e., it was not insolence or presumption which led him astray.
65. I.e., can cause night to fall.
66. Si-nuhe maintains the flattering pretense that he has been ruling his
part of Retenu on behalf of Pharaoh.

my eldest son being responsible for my tribe. My tribe and all
my property were in his charge: my serfs, all my cattle, my
fruit, and every pleasant tree of mine.

Then this servant came southward. I halted at the "Ways of
Horus."[67] The commander there who was responsible for the
patrol sent a message to the Residence to make (it) known.
Then his majesty sent a capable overseer of peasants of the
palace, with loaded ships in his train, carrying presentations
from the royal presence FOR THE ASIATICS WHO HAD FOLLOWED
ME, ESCORTING ME TO THE "WAYS OF HORUS." I called each of
them by his name.[68] Every butler was (busy) at his duties.
When I started and set sail, the kneading and straining (of
beer) was carried on beside me, until I had reached the town
of Lisht.[69]

When day had broken, very early, they came and summoned
me, ten men coming and ten men going to usher me to the palace.[70] I put my brow to the ground between the sphinxes,[71]
while the royal children were waiting in a *recess* to meet me.
The courtiers who usher into the audience hall set me on the
way to the private chambers. I found his majesty upon the
Great Throne in a *recess* of fine gold. When I was stretched out
upon my belly, I knew not myself in his presence,[72] (although)
this god greeted me pleasantly. I was like a man caught in the
dark: my soul departed, my body was powerless, my heart was
not in my body, that I might know life from death.

THEN HIS MAJESTY SAID TO ONE OF THESE COURTIERS: "Lift
him up. Let him speak to me." Then his majesty said: "Behold,
thou art come. Thou hast trodden the foreign countries *and
made a flight.* (But now) elderliness has attacked thee; thou
hast reached old age. It is no small matter that thy corpse be
(properly) buried; thou shouldst not be interred by bowmen.[73]
Do not, do not act thus any longer: (for) thou dost not speak

67. The Egyptian frontier station facing Sinai.
68. He paid the Asiatics the compliment of introducing them to Pharaoh.
69. The capital at that time, some distance south of the later Memphis.
70. Ten men were assigned to summon him and ten to escort him.
71. Or statues.
72. I.e., "I lost my presence of mind."
73. Foreigners.

when thy name is pronounced!" Yet (I) was afraid to respond,
and I answered it with the answer of one afraid: "What is it
that my lord says to me? I should answer it, (but) there is nothing that I can do: it is really the hand of a god. It is a terror that
is in my belly like that which produced the fated flight. BEHOLD,
I AM BEFORE THEE. THINE IS LIFE. MAY THY MAJESTY DO AS HE
PLEASES."

THEREUPON the royal children WERE ushered in. Then his
majesty said to the Queen: "Here is Si-nuhe, come as a Bedu,[74]
(in) the guise of the Asiatics." She gave a very great cry, and
the royal children clamored all together. Then they said to his
majesty: "It is not really he, O Sovereign, my lord!" Then his
majesty said: "It is really he!"[75] Now when they had brought
with them their bead-necklaces, their rattles, and their sistra,
then they presented them to his majesty.[76] ". . . Loose the horn
of thy bow and relax thy arrow![77] Give breath to him that was
stifled! Give us our goodly gift in this sheikh Si-Mehit,[78] a bowman born in Egypt. He made a flight through fear of thee; he
left the land through terror of thee. (But) the face of him who
beholds thy face shall not *blench*; the eye which looks at thee
shall not be afraid!"

Then his majesty said: "He shall not fear. He has no *title* to
be in dread. He shall be a courtier among the nobles. He shall
be put in the ranks of the courtiers. Proceed ye to the inner
chambers of the *morning (toilet)*, in order to make his position."[79]

So I went forth from the midst of the inner chambers, with
the royal children giving me their hands. Thereafter we went to
the Great Double Door. I was put into the house of a royal son,
in which were splendid things. A cool room was in it, and im-

74. Bedouin.
75. They do not recognize the formerly elegant courtier in the wild
Bedouin.
76. Rattles and sistra: musical instruments. The large necklaces are the
symbols of their goddess, Hathor (ancient sky-goddess and goddess of
women). By reaching out these instruments to someone during a dance, the
women thereby present him with the goddess's blessing.
77. I.e., set the man free.
78. A designation of Si-nuhe, on his return from Asia, as "Son of the
North Wind."
79. Si-nuhe's new rank is to be established by a change of dress.

ages of the horizon.[80] Costly things of the Treasury were in it. Clothing of royal linen, myrrh, and prime oil of the king and of the nobles whom he loves were in every room. Every butler was (busy) at his duties. Years were made to pass away from my body. I was *plucked*, and my hair was combed. A load (of dirt) was given to the desert, and my clothes (to) the Sand-Crossers. I was clad in fine linen and anointed with prime oil. I slept on a bed, I gave up the sand to them who are in it, and wood oil to him who is anointed with it. I was given a house *which had a garden*, which had been in the possession of a courtier. Many *craftsmen* built it, and all its wood(work) was newly restored. Meals were brought to me from the palace three or four times a day, apart from that which the royal children gave, without ceasing a moment.

There was constructed for me a pyramid-tomb of stone in the midst of the pyramid-tombs.[81] The stone-masons who hew a pyramid-tomb took over its ground-area. The outline-draftsmen designed in it; the chief sculptors carved in it; and the overseers of works who are in the necropolis made it their concern.[82] Its necessary materials were made from all the outfittings which are placed at a tomb-shaft.[83] Mortuary priests were given to me. There was made for me a necropolis garden, with fields in it *formerly (extending)* as far as the town, like that which is done for a chief courtier. My statue[84] was overlaid with gold, and its skirt was of fine gold. It was his majesty who had it made. There is no poor man for whom the like has been done.

(So) I was under the favor of the king's presence until the day of mooring had come.[85]

IT HAS COME (TO ITS END), FROM BEGINNING TO END AS IT HAD BEEN FOUND IN WRITING.

80. Painted decorations. The "cool room" may have been a bathroom or a cellar for preserving foods.
81. The members of Pharaoh's court are buried around his grave.
82. I.e., the best craftsmen who work on the royal pyramids are also employed on the pyramid of Si-nuhe.
83. I.e., the various offerings which a well-equipped tomb of this period contained.
84. The statue erected in his tomb.
85. I.e., the day of death.

Introduction to The Teaching of Amenophis

"The Teaching of Amenophis" belongs to a genre—so-called wisdom literature—of which examples survive from very ancient times. Amenophis, like other Egyptian authors of similar works, was a royal official writing to advise posterity on how to succeed in the world. He was obviously a man of some importance, possessing sepulchral monuments in two cities, though whether he was the land- and corn-administrator for all Egypt or just for the district around Abydos in Middle Egypt is not clear. His young son, to whom the teaching is directed, had already entered upon a priestly career in the temple of Panopolis.

The Amenophis text as now extant probably dates from around the Twenty-fifth Dynasty (ca 700 B.C.). In several respects it differs from its predecessors in Egyptian literature. It is arranged in separate lines of poetry and divided into numbered chapters, which is unusual in Egypt. The poetical effect is produced by parallelism, rather than rhyme; the lines are organized chiefly in couplets or quatrains. The ethical emphasis of Amenophis' teaching is also unusual. Though he does not neglect to include the usual advice on how to please one's superiors and advance in the royal service, his concern for personal character and moral rectitude is even stronger. The teaching is full of religious piety: he alludes to the old myths and sometimes speaks of God in general, rather than any particular deity, leading some authorities to declare him a monotheist. His ideal is the tranquil man, pious, benevolent, and content with his lot in life, as opposed to the "passionate" man, ambitious, obtrusive, and dishonest.

Various scholars have remarked upon the extraordinary resemblances between "The Teaching of Amenophis" and the Old Testament Book of Proverbs, suggesting that one must have borrowed from the other. Perhaps at one time there existed a Hebrew or Aramaic translation of Amenophis' work, which the Hebrew compiler of Proverbs utilized and adapted to his own purposes. Such an assumption is not without foundation; for we know that in the period when the Hebrews were transforming themselves from a nomadic into a settled people under King Saul and his successors,*

* See Vol. II of this series, Sec. I, Part 5: "The Hebrews."

they looked especially to Egypt and Babylonia for instruction in the arts of civilization. Educated foreigners familiar with the ways of the great world were not lacking among them—for example, King Hezekiah's scribe Shebna. To be sure, some of the similarities between the Egyptian and the Hebrew work are of a type found in the didactic literature of many lands and peoples. Others, however, offer such striking parallels that the assumption of a connection between them is hard to avoid.

Perhaps both Amenophis and the compiler of Proverbs borrowed from some earlier common source, now unknown to us; for much of the wisdom of the ancient Near East was certainly international in character. Various passages throughout the Old Testament recall "The Teaching of Amenophis," though it is in the Book of Proverbs that the resemblances are most evident. Especially in the third section (Prov. 22:17–24:22), the evidence for a connection is strong. In the ancient Hebrew ("Massoretic") Bible, this third section bears the title, "The Words of the Wise." Here the parallels with the Egyptian work are numerous and close, often employing identical figures of speech and appearing in the same order and context.

The text of "The Teaching of Amenophis" has fortunately survived in its entirety. Translation, however, offers particular difficulties. The "Teaching" is consciously artificial in form and expression, using rare and poetical words; the phraseology is concise and sometimes obscure; sentences are short and disconnected. It also shows considerable evidence of scribal errors, making the translation of many passages only tentative.

THE TEACHING OF AMENOPHIS

Preface

A. THE BOOK

1   Beginning of teaching how to live,
          guidance for welfare;

From "The Teaching of Amenophis," F. Ll. Griffith, ed. and trans., *Journal of Egyptian Archaeology*, XII (1926), 195-224. Reprinted by permission of the Egypt Exploration Society.
     The left-hand numerals indicate the pages of the papyrus on which the Egyptian text is written. Conventional line numbers appear on the right.

every direction for intercourse with elders,
    rules for (intercourse with ?) courtiers;
knowledge how to answer a statement to its pronouncer,[1] 5
    and return a report to one that has sent him;[2]

to direct him to the path of life,
    and make him prosper upon earth;
to let his heart enter its shrine,[3]
    and steer it (?) clear of evil;   10
to save him from the mouth of others,
    praised in the mouth of men.

B. THE AUTHOR

Made by a superintendent of the soil, experienced in his
    office,
    the fruit of a scribe of Egypt.[4]
Superintendent of cereals,[5] regulating the *waze*-measure,[6] 15
    who ordained the corn-yield (?) for his lord.

Who inscribed islands and new lands in the great name
    of His Majesty,
    and set a land-mark at the boundary of the sown;
2   who safeguarded the king by his markings
    and made the terrier[7] of the Black Land.

Scribe establishing divine endowments of all the gods,
    giver of leases to other people.[8]

1. The real meaning seems to be: "to rebut an accuser."
2. Compare Proverbs 22:21 ". . . that thou mightest answer the words of truth to them that send unto thee?"
3. I.e., to enable him to retain his presence of mind, or to judge accurately.
4. This phrase probably means that the Teaching itself is the product of an Egyptian scribe, though it may also refer to the author as the son of a scribe.
5. May be a poetic version of Amenophis' official title.
6. This is the corn-measure which played so large a part in the life of an Egyptian scribe. *Waze* means "eye of Horus" or "eye of Re," i.e., the god was believed to oversee the honesty of the weights and measures and prevent falsification.
7. The book in which the details of landholdings are recorded.
8. The preceding six lines evidently record some of Amenophis' functions as superintendent of lands.

Superintendent of cereals, provider (?) of food,   5
    transporting (?) magazine(s) (?) of (?) cereals.

Tranquil indeed in Thinite Tew-wer,[9]
    justified in A-pe;[10]
possessing a pyramid-tomb on the west of Sen-ut,[11]
    possessing a sepulchre in Abydos.[12]   10
Amenemopi[13] son of Kanakht,
    justified in Tew-wer.

C. THE PERSON TO WHOM THE TEACHING WAS ADDRESSED

(for) his son, the youngest of his children,
    little compared to his relations;
over the mysteries of Min Kamephis (i.e., Bull of his
                Mother),   15
    water-pourer of Wennofri;[14]
who installs Horus[15] upon the throne of his father,
    his (?) guardian (?) in his noble shrine;
fuller (?) [of the garments of Isis?][16] the Great,

3   watcher (?) of the Mother of God;
inspector of the black kine of the terrace of Min,[17]
    protecting Min in his shrine;
Harmakher[18] his true name,
    child of a nobleman of A-pe: 5
son of the sistrum-player of Shu and Tefnut,[19]
    chief cymbalist of Horus, Tewosri.

9. The sacred quarter of the city of Thinis.
10. The city of Panopolis.
11. A name for Panopolis, or a temple in that city. Since Panopolis was on
the east bank of the Nile, "west of Sen-ut" seems to indicate some place on
the opposite side of the river (probably on the edge of the desert where
cemeteries usually lay).
12. The sacred city of the god Osiris in Middle Egypt.
13. Probably the same name as Amen-opi (Amenophis).
14. A name for Osiris.
15. The ancient sky- and sun-god, son of Isis and Osiris.
16. Mother of Horus (see following line).
17. A fertility god also identified with Horus.
18. The name of the young son, meaning "Horus justified."
19. The god and goddess of the atmosphere and of moisture, respectively.

CHAPTER I   CHARGE TO THE PUPIL

He saith: First Chapter:
Give thine ears, hear (the words) that are said,[20]
    give thy mind to interpret them;[21]   10
to put them in thy heart is good,
    (but there is) woe to him who neglecteth them;
let them rest in the casket of thy belly,[22]
    that they may be the threshold (?) in thy heart;[23]
verily (?) when there cometh a gale of speech,   15
    they will be a mooring-post in (?) thy tongue.[24]

If thou spend thy life-time with these things in thy heart,
    thou wilt find it a success;
4   thou wilt find my words a storehouse of life,
    and thy body will prosper upon earth.

CHAPTER II   HUMANITY, AND VARIOUS ADVICE

Second Chapter:
Beware of robbing a poor wretch,
    of being valorous against the man of broken arm.[25]   5
Put not forth thine hand to touch an old man,
    nor snatch (?) at the word of the aged.[26]
Let not thyself be sent on a wicked mission,
    nor desire (the company of) him that hath per-
        formed it.

20. Compare Proverbs 22:17: "Bow down thine ear, and hear the words of the wise, and apply thine heart unto my knowledge."
21. Compare Proverbs 1:6: "To understand a proverb, and the interpretation; the words of the wise, and their dark sayings." I.e., sages love obscurity.
22. Common expression for "inmost soul."
23. Compare Proverbs 6:21: "Bind them [the laws] continually upon thine heart, and tie them about thy neck."
24. Compare Proverbs 22:18: "For it is a pleasant thing if thou keep them [the words of the wise] within thee; they shall withal be fitted in thy lips."
25. An expression for weakness and helplessness. Compare Proverbs 22:22: "Rob not the poor, because he is poor: neither oppress the afflicted in the gate."
26. I.e., do not be too forward in addressing the old or the great.

Clamour not against him whom thou hast injured,   10
  nor return him an answer to justify (?) thyself.

Him who hath done ill, the quay slips away (?) from
  him,[27]
  his wetted land, it (?) carries him away;
the north wind cometh down to end his hour,
  it uniteth with the tempest;   15
the thunder is loud, the crocodiles are vicious.
  Thou passionate man, what is thy condition?
He cries out, his voice (reacheth) to heaven.
  Thou Moon, bring forward his crime![28]

5 Steer that we may carry the bad man over,
  for we will not do as he (hath done).[29]
Lift him up, give him thy hand,
  commit him to the arms of God;
fill his belly with bread of thine,   5
  that he may be satisfied and understand (?).[30]

Another thing good in the heart of God
  is to pause before speaking.

CHAPTER III PRUDENCE IN ARGUMENT

Third Chapter:
Do not join wrangling with the hot-mouthed,   10
  nor goad him with words.
Pause before an intruder,
  and give way unto him that attacketh.
Sleep a night before speaking;
  the storm, it bursts forth like flame in straw.

27. Meaning obscure.
28. A technical term for "impeachment" or "accusation of crime." This
section appears to describe the plight of the evil man at the point of death:
the moon is called upon to accuse him before Osiris.
29. Compare Proverbs 24:29: "Say not, I will do so to him as he hath done
to me: I will render to the man according to his work."
30. I.e., be kind to the evil-doer in distress. Compare Proverbs 25:21: "If
thine enemy be hungry, give him bread to eat; and if he be thirsty, give
him water to drink."

The passionate man in his hour[31]   15
    withdraw thyself before him;
leave him to his own devices;
    God will know how to reply to him.

If thou spend thy life-time with these things in thy heart,
    thy children shall see them.

CHAPTER IV   THE PASSIONATE MAN AND THE TRANQUIL MAN

Fourth Chapter: 20
6   As to the passionate man in the temple,
        he is like a tree grown in the forest (?);
    in a moment comes its loss of foliage;
        its end is reached in the dock-yard (?);[32]
    or (?) it is floated far from its place,   5
        the flame is its winding-sheet.

The truly tranquil man, he setteth himself aside,
    he is like a tree grown in a plot (?);
it grows green, it doubles its yield,
    it (stands) in front of its lord,   10
its fruit is sweet, its shade is pleasant,
    and its end is reached in the garden.[33]

CHAPTER V   HONESTY AND TRANQUILITY IN THE TEMPLE

Fifth Chapter:
Misuse (?) not the shares of the temple,
    be not greedy, (thus) wilt thou find excess (beyond
        your expectation),   15
    remove not a servant of a god,
        in order to do a benefit to another.

31. A common expression, meaning when his characteristic tendencies are
stirred.
32. The passionate man is compared to a wild tree, which is used in ship-
building or burned for charcoal.
33. Note the analogous contrast applied to the godly and the ungodly man in
Psalm 1:3-4: "And he [the godly man] shall be like a tree planted by the
rivers of water, that bringeth forth his fruit in his season; his leaf also
shall not wither; and whatsoever he doeth shall prosper. The ungodly are
not so: but are like the chaff which the wind driveth away."

Say not "to-day is as to-morrow";
    how will these things end?

7   The morrow is come, to-day is gone,
    the deep hath become the edge of the waves,
the crocodiles are uncovered, the hippopotami on dry land,
    the fishes gasping (?);
the jackals are sated, the wild-fowl in festival,   5
    the nets are empty (?).

As to all the tranquil in the temple,
    they say "Great is the good pleasure of Re,"[34]
Hold fast to the tranquil man, (thus) wilt thou find life,
    (and) thy body shall prosper upon earth.

CHAPTER VI   ENCROACHMENT ON THE LAND OF OTHERS

Sixth Chapter:
Remove not the landmark on the boundaries of the sown,[35]
    nor shift the position of the measuring-cord;
covet not a cubit of land,
    nor throw down the boundaries of the widow.   15

The rut of trampling (?), the wear of time,
    he who wrongfully seizes it in the field,[36]
if (?) he snare by false oaths,
    is lassoed by the Power of the Moon.[37]

8   Mark well him who hath done this on earth,
    for he is an oppressor of the weak,
he is an enemy working destruction within thee,
    deprival of life in his eye,
his house is an enemy to the town;   5
    (but) his barns are destroyed,

---

34. I.e., the important thing is to please Re.
35. Compare Proverbs 22:28: "Remove not the ancient landmark, which thy fathers have set."
36. Or: "that which thou hath seized wrongfully."
37. Compare Proverbs 23:10-11: "Remove not the old landmark: and enter not into the fields of the fatherless: For their redeemer is mighty; he shall plead their cause with thee."

his goods are taken out of the hand of his children,
    and his property is given to another.

Beware of throwing down the boundaries of the sown,
    lest a terror carry thee away;   10
a man propitiates God by the Power of the Lord,[38]
    when he defines the boundaries of the sown.

Desire then to make thine own self prosperous;
    beware of the Universal Lord;[39]
trample not the furrow of another,   15
    it is good for thee to be sound in regard to them.

Cultivate the fields, that thou mayest find what thou
    needest;
    and receive the bread of thine own threshing-floor;
better is a bushel that God giveth thee
    than five thousand (obtained) by force;   20
9   they stay not a day in store and barn,
    they make no food in the beer-jar;
a moment is their duration in the granary,
    when morning cometh they have gone below.

Better is poverty at the hand of God   5
    than riches in the storehouse;
better is bread with happy heart
    than riches with vexation.[40]

CHAPTER VII   THE SEARCH FOR WEALTH

Seventh Chapter:
Cast not thy heart after riches;   10

38. Perhaps "the power of the owner of the property," i.e. the magic power conferred by ownership.
39. One of several Egyptian expressions for a deity, without specifying the name of any particular one.
40. Compare Proverbs 15:16-17: "Better is little with the fear of the Lord than great treasure and trouble therewith. Better is a dinner of herbs where love is, than a stalled ox and hatred therewith." Also Proverbs 17:1: "Better is a dry morsel, and quietness therewith, than an house full of sacrifices with strife."

there is no ignoring of Shay and Renent.[41]
Place not for thyself thy thoughts (on things) outside;
    every man is (destined) for his hour.

Labour not to seek increase,[42]
    (then ?) thy needs shall be secure for thee;   15
if riches be brought to thee by robbery,
    they shall not stay the night with thee;
day dawneth and they are not in thy house,
    their places shall be seen, but they are not (there);
(perchance) the earth hath opened its mouth, "It adjusts
        it and swallows it,"[43]   20
10   and has sunk them in Tei,[44]
(or) they have made for themselves a great breach of
        their measure,[45]
    and they have sunk themselves in the corn-store,
(or) they have made themselves wings like geese,
    they have flown to heaven.[46]   5

Rejoice not thyself (because of) riches by robbery,
    nor groan over poverty;
when an archer in front pushes forward (?)
    his troop leaves him (in difficulty);
the boat of the covetous is left (in) the mud,   10
    while the bark of the tranquil sails (with the breeze).

Thou shalt pray to the Aten[47] when he rises,
    saying "Grant me prosperity and health,"
and he will give thee thy needs in life,
    and thou wilt be safe from fear.   15

41. The god and goddess of Fate.
42. Compare Proverbs 23:4: "Labour not to be rich: cease from thine own wisdom."
43. If the translation is correct, this must be an old phrase describing the voracious mouth of the earth.
44. The Underworld.
45. Or perhaps: "a great cavern of their size."
46. Compare Proverbs 23:5: ". . . for riches certainly make themselves wings; they fly away as an eagle toward heaven."
47. The sun's disk.

Eighth Chapter:
Set thy goodness in the bowels of men[48]
        that everyone salute thee;
(for) one acclaims the Uraeus,[49]
        and spits on the Apophis-serpent.[50]   20

Keep sound thy tongue from words of detraction;
11   (thus) wilt thou be the favourite of the others,
    thou wilt find thy place within the temple,
        and thy provisions in the bread-offerings of thy lord;
    thou wilt be revered in old age and be hidden (in) thy
            coffin,
        and be safe from the Power of God.   5

Cry not "crime" at a man;
        hide the manner of (a fugitive's) flight.
If thou hearest (to judge ?) a thing that may be either
            good or bad,
        do this outside, (where) it is not heard;
put a good report upon thy tongue,   10
        while the ill is hidden in thy belly.[51]

17   Fifteenth Chapter:
Do well that thou mayest reach what I (?) am;[52]   5
        do not ink a pen to do an injury.
The beak of the Ibis[53] is the finger of the scribe;
        beware of disturbing it.

48. I.e., accustom men to have a good opinion of thee in their inmost soul,
or "belly."
49. The serpent which the sun-god and the king wore as a diadem.
50. The cloud-dragon who threatens the sun. I.e., both the Uraeus and the
Apophis are dangerous serpents, but one is praised and the other execrated.
51. Compare Proverbs 24:11: "If thou forbear to deliver them that are
drawn unto death, and those that are ready to be slain . . ."
52. Or: "a certain rank," or "an assured condition."
53. The sacred heron, a manifestation of the scribe-god, Thoth.

The Ape[54] dwelleth in the House of Khmûn,[55]
    (but) his eye travels round the Two Lands;   10
if he sees him that perverts with his finger,
    he takes away his provisions in the deep waters.
As for a scribe who perverts with his finger,
    his son shall not be registered.

If thou spend thy life-time with these things in thy heart,   15
    thy children shall see them.

CHAPTER XVI   FALSE WEIGHTS AND SHAM

Sixteenth Chapter:
Tamper not with the scales, nor falsify the *kite*-weights,
    nor diminish the fractions of the corn-measure.[56]
Desire not the corn-measure of the fields,   20
    and then neglect those of the Treasury.

The Ape sitteth by the balance,[57]
18   his heart being the plummet.
Where is a god so great as Thoth,
    he that discovered these things, to make them?

Fashion not for thyself deficient *kite*-weights;
    they abound in armies (?)[58] by the Power of God.   5
If thou seest another perverting,
    thou shalt pass by him at a distance.

Covet not copper,
    avoid beautiful linen;

54. Symbol of Thoth, the god of scribes, of invention and learning.
55. Hermopolis, the city of Thoth.
56. Compare Proverbs 20:23: "Divers weights are an abomination unto the Lord; and a false balance is not good." Also Proverbs 20:10: "Divers weights, and divers measures, both of them are alike abomination to the Lord."
57. Compare Proverbs 16:11: "A just weight and balance are the Lord's: all the weights of the bag are his work."
58. This must mean that the weights have armies to defend them, thanks to Thoth.

what is the good of it, a cloak of *mek?*   10
 when it is a perversion before God.
if gold-bases (?)[59] be overlaid (?) to (appear as) pure
 gold (?)
  at dawn it is of lead.

19

CHAPTER XVIII   OVER-ANXIETY

Eighteenth Chapter: 10
Lay thee not down at night fearing the morrow;
 when day appears, what is the morrow like?
Man knoweth not how the morrow will be,
  (The events of the morrow are in the hand of God);

God is (ever) in his success,
 Man is (ever) in his failure.[60]   15
The words which men say are one thing,
 The things which God doeth are another.[61]

Say not "I have no crime,"
 nor labour to seek strife (*sic*).[62]
Crime belongeth to God,   20
 it is sealed with his finger.

There is no success with God,
 nor is there failure before him;
20 if he turn him to seek success,
  in a moment the man (?) mars it.

Be resolute in thy heart, make firm thy mind;
 steer not with (?) thy tongue;

59. This might be an expression for stucco, bronze, or other material used as a basis for gilding.
60. Compare Proverbs 19:21: "There are many devices in a man's heart; nevertheless the counsel of the Lord, that shall stand."
61. Compare Proverbs 16:9: "A man's heart deviseth his way; but the Lord directeth his steps," from which is derived the maxim: "Man proposes, God disposes."
62. "Strife" (with God) or "confusion"? Meaning uncertain.

    the tongue of a man is the rudder of a boat,   5
        (but) the Universal Lord is its pilot.

CHAPTER XXI   RETICENCE

21   Twenty-first Chapter:
22   Say not "Find me a strong chief,
        for a man in thy city hath injured me";
   say not "Find me a redeemer,
        for a man who hateth me hath injured me."

   Verily thou knowest not the designs of God,   5
        thou canst not realise (?) the morrow.[63]
   Sit thee down at the hands of God;
        thy tranquillity will overthrow them.[64]

   Verily a crocodile which is void of proclaiming,[65]
        inveterate is the dread of it.   10

   Empty not thine inmost soul to everybody,
        nor spoil (thereby) thine influence;[66]
   spread not thy sayings about to others,
        nor associate to thyself one who lays bare his heart.[67]

   Better is a man that (hides) his report within himself   15
        than he who tells a thing to disadvantage.[68]
   One does not run to reach perfection;
        one does not throw (?)[69] to injure himself (?).

63. Compare Proverbs 27:1: "Boast not thyself of to morrow; for thou knowest not what a day may bring forth."
64. Compare Proverbs 20:22: "Say not thou, I will recompense evil; but wait on the Lord, and he shall save thee."
65. "Void of proclaiming": an artificial literary expression, meaning "sound-less" or "dumb."
66. Compare Proverbs 23:9: "Speak not in the ears of a fool: for he will despise the wisdom of thy words."
67. Compare Proverbs 20:19: "He that goeth about as a tale-bearer revealeth secrets: therefore meddle not with him that flattereth with his lips."
68. Compare Proverbs 12:23: "A prudent man concealeth knowledge: but the heart of fools proclaimeth foolishness."
69. Perhaps "invent" instead of "throw."

CHAPTER XXVI   CONDUCT TOWARDS SENIORS IN SOCIETY

24   Twenty-sixth Chapter:
Sit not in the beer-house,
25   and then join (?) one senior to thyself,
whether he be young (but) great in his office,
     or old by birth;
associate with thyself a man of thine own rank;
     Re is helpful from afar.   5

(But) if thou see one greater than thyself outside
     and attendants following him, do (him?) reverence;
give a hand to an old man when he is sated with beer,
     reverence (?) (him) as (?) his children (would).

The strong arm is not softened (?) by being uncovered;   10
     the back is not broken by bending it;
poverty will not be made for a man when he says the
       pleasant thing,
     any more than riches when his speech is straw (?).[70]

A pilot who sees from afar,
     he will not make his boat a wreck.

CHAPTER XXVII   SUBMISSION TO THE OLD

Twenty-seventh Chapter:
Curse not one older than thou,
     for he hath seen Re before thee;
cause him not to accuse thee to the Aten at its rising,
     saying "Another, a youth, hath cursed an old man";   20
very painful before Re
26   is a youth who curses an old man.

Let him beat thee, with thy hand in thy bosom;
     let him curse thee, while thou keepest silence.
If next day thou come before him,

70. Perhaps meaning "dry and harsh."

he will give thee bread without stint.   5
The food of a hound is (the affair) of his master,
    and he barks unto him that gives it.

CHAPTER XXX   EPILOGUE

27   Thirtieth Chapter:
See for thyself these thirty chapters,
    they please, they educate;
they are the foremost of all books;
    they instruct the ignorant.   10
If they be read before the ignorant,
    he will be cured (?) by reason of them.
Fill thyself with them; put them in thy heart,
    and be an interpreter of them, explaining as a
        teacher.   15

As to a scribe who is experienced in his office,
    he will find himself worthy (?) to be a courtier.[71]

---

71. Compare Proverbs 22:29: "Seest thou a man diligent in his business? he shall stand before kings; he shall not stand before mean [i.e., obscure] men."